BRAVE NEW
META WORLD

Amina Qureshi
Dona Varghese

FIRST PRINTING, December 2022.
Harry Markos, Director.

Paperback: ISBN 978-1-915387-54-7
eBook: ISBN 978-1-915387-55-4

Book design by: Ian Sharman
Cover design by: Tanya Khosla

www.markosia.com

First Edition

ACKNOWLEDGMENTS

When asked what I wanted to be when I grew up, I always said "an author" - even when I was too small to understand what that meant, or the amount of energy and creative prowess it would require to publish a book. But most importantly, I never appreciated the amount of people who would inspire and push me to publish *Brave New Meta World*.

To **Dona Varghese**, an old-time colleague, friend, and co-author. Writing this with you has shown me how friendship can make a complex and stressful process like writing a book fun and fulfilling. You were one of the first to teach me the fundamentals of media, to accelerate my thinking by layering in academia and you consistently continue to challenge my thinking. For this, I am indebted to you.

To **Andrew Mattern** and **Harris Mattern**, thanks for giving me the space to embark on this creative journey. You provide me so much joy and fulfilment in my life, you are the fuel behind the energy that I bring into every single day. Your love and warmth and support are the bedrocks of my success, both personally and professionally.

To my **colleagues**, past and present, you have inspired me to think about the advertising space differently. First you taught me the basics of our industry, then you taught me to critique it, and finally - you taught me to embrace and love it. I am only this passionate because I've been privileged enough to work with you.

To the significant **thought leaders** in this space: Scott Galloway, Kara Swisher, Tristan Harris, Chamath Palihapitiya, Tim Wu, Charles Warner, David Carroll, David Lieberman, Rory Sutherland, Frances Haugen. Your commitment to bringing transparency and accountability into this space is commendable.

To my **Mother, Father & Brother**: I would never have been challenged to think the way that I do without the experiences of living across so many cultures. You taught me to take all the bits that are interesting and string them together to make sense of this world. To my **extended family**: you instilled in me a deep love and appreciation for family.

To my **friends**: in many ways, you've assumed the role of my family. Living in different corners of the world with you - whether in Paris, London, Kuala Lumpur, Vancouver, Montreal, or Toronto - has been the experience of a lifetime.

— *Amina Qureshi*

Winston Churchill once said, "Writing a book is an adventure. To begin with it is a toy and an amusement. Then it becomes a mistress, then it becomes a master, then it becomes a tyrant. The last phase is that just as you are about to be reconciled to your servitude, you kill the monster and fling him to the public."

Brave New Meta World is a collaborative piece that has been in the making for close to a decade. It took us seventeen months to put it down on paper, but we started this journey much before that. This book is an average of countless hours of talking about our work, living in and studying the industry we are part of and pondering over how to live in this fast- paced tech world. It is impossible to thank individually the huge number of people who have contributed to the creation of Brave New Meta World. All I can do here is signal a few who have been particularly helpful.

To **Amina Qureshi**, my co-author, who encouraged me to come out of my shell. You are all the good things in this world. You taught me that being worldly is a niche. Writing this book with you was such a pleasure, it felt like we were on a 17-months' vacation! Your unique and bold perspective on life is what this world needs more of. It's been a privilege and thank you for being a constant inspiration.

To **Navroop K Chari** & **Swathi Eapen**, my soul sisters. Thank you for accepting me – all of me. Your patience and unconditional love have nurtured my growth in more ways than you know.

To my **Friends,** who I met in Dubai, Kochi, Pune, Bombay, Pretoria, and New York, are an extension of my best self. Thank you for all the laughter we have shared over the years, across different time zones. I would like to give a special shout out to **Paulina Kay**, **Janaa Murad** & **Jos Dirkx** for the support you provided, without any hesitance.

To **Daniel Vaczi**, **Mehdy Mamode** & **Mayank Garg**, my peer friends. Thank you for giving me all the opportunities and believing in my potential before I did. I love what I do because of you.

To my **Collaborators** at DV Media Co. Thank you for believing in my vision. Thank you for helping me implement my vision. Thank you for supporting me through this journey of writing Brave New Meta World. I would like to give a special shout out to **Tanya Khosla** & **Rose Davis** for the indescribable support you provided.

To the **Varghese Family**, my lifeline. Thank you for constantly reminding me I am so much more than I give myself credit for.

— *Dona Varghese*

CONTENTS

Prologue: Why it Matters Now
Amina Qureshi
Dona Varghese

"If a business is built on misleading users on data exploitation, on choices that are no choices at all, then it does not deserve our praise. It deserves reform."
- Tim Cook

If you take away anything from this book, let it be how to become a better, more discerning thinker.

Throughout this book, we will uncover some truths about the advertising industry and its evolution, the important role that brands and agencies play in shaping the future of this industry and what power – us as, end consumers – can exercise to ensure we leave our society in a better, more educated, and more informed place. At a time when we are at a crossroads in marketing, at the intersection of data, technology, and privacy – we must collectively decide to steer the $500 Billion-dollar advertising behemoth in the right direction. Why does it matter now? Marketing has existed for decades and has never had to rely on hundreds of data points stitched across various platforms to succeed.

But now, increasingly, there is a moment of pause where we must think of the implications of conducting a Google Search or scrolling endlessly through Instagram. It's a moment to contemplate whether the immediacy of social media will have long-standing effects on the way our brains function and operate. Surely comparing ourselves to the best, most unrealistic versions of celebrities or even our own peer groups can't be healthy. If there are studies to suggest that there are harmful secondary effects of a platform like Instagram, shouldn't more people care about it?

It turns out, the answer isn't so simple. When we set out to write this book, our ideas around how the ad world operated, or what made certain platforms more questionable than others – were born out of casual social conversations we would have during the pandemic. Both being passionate proponents of the advertising industry, we came to know and love an industry that had somehow changed over the years. The promise of digital advertising had evolved into a constant stream of headlines in the news. Headlines around data, privacy, and consumer mistrust. And at the forefront of these headlines, was always Facebook. I felt this constant tension: on one hand, I was an avid Instagram user myself and on the other, I helped brands to successfully navigate and advertise on it. I felt uneasy over Facebook's practices from the beginning but speaking to Dona Varghese reaffirmed the notion that perhaps there was far more to Facebook's impact socially, politically, and culturally than we had realized.

In an early 2021 speech to commemorate International Data Privacy Day, Apple's CEO Tim Cook took to the stage to publicly address Facebook's questionable use of its user data. During his speech, Cook says, "we've arrived at a nexus in time where we must acknowledge that the path of least resistance is rarely the path of wisdom. If a business is built on misleading users with data exploitation, on choices that are not choices at all, then it does not deserve our praise. It deserves reform."

The incidents that preceded or followed Facebook's use of its first party data were increasingly global in nature. News feeds in markets like the Philippines were being filled with fake news, swaying public perception, and fuelling modern ethnic cleansing in Myanmar. At times, it felt like these incidents *couldn't* possibly be real. Perhaps some evil dictator had managed to hack the system and got away with it, but Facebook couldn't willingly be involved at a more systemic level by turning a blind eye to known events. But time and time again, news would break around Facebook's continued involvement in data leaks and privacy breaches.

In late 2020, the Netflix documentary The Social Dilemma broke, and ex-Google ethicist Tristan Harris was gaining increased notoriety for his work around marketing and ethics. He referred extensively to the work of Tim Wu and specifically to his book, *The Attention Merchants* which speaks at length about our attention as being the last frontier to be hijacked by social media companies. It's a beautiful reflection on an emerging strain of anxiety about the information age that we find ourselves in. And it was during this time that Varghese and I again spurred conversations around how many people – end users of Instagram but also those working within the advertising industry – were simply unaware of the many underpinnings of how Facebook evolved and grew.

Social media as a tactic to reach mass swaths of the population is a relatively new phenomenon in the scope of communications platforms. As Marshall McLuhan put it "The medium is the message" so we must first understand what message is being conveyed by Facebook and Instagram as platforms. It's a relatively passive experience for users who find themselves endlessly scrolling, it's an opportunity for brands to hopefully reach relevant audiences and convert them into customers and it's an engine that is feeding Facebook back a gold mine in first party data on user behavior and preferences.

But why does it matter now? It matters now because we are sitting at a critical junction of misinformation fuelled by Facebook's complex algorithm.

We increasingly have a deep yearning for the truth at a time when almost 70% of Americans cite social media as a main source for news. If newsfeeds are being poisoned by fake engagement, prioritizing content that is hateful and incendiary, then how are we meant to discern facts and reality from nonsense? Younger generations are seeking radical transparency and are therefore turning to platforms that prioritize privacy. Lawmakers are understanding that it's no longer acceptable to turn to antiquated Internet legislation to absolve Facebook of any sort of accountability. Brands like Patagonia are beginning to pull every last advertising dollar from Facebook as their stance against the way the company continues to operate, changes.

Only with a critical eye are we able to affect the change that we need as we ready ourselves for the next phase of the Internet evolution, the meta world. This doesn't mean we throw our phones into the abyss and turn to a life of complete solitude, but it does require us to observe and understand our relationship with social media in a more thoughtful way. As Tim Cook insinuates, perhaps now is the deciding moment to criticize the theory of technology which asserts that "all engagement is good engagement".

The human brain was not made to evolve quickly and it's a particularly vulnerable organ to hijack, with social algorithms only getting stronger and smarter. When I, Dona Varghese, go for a walk most evenings, my phone is tucked neatly in my pocket. I check my step count and normally listen to podcasts. Over time, I noticed the algorithm on my streaming app catering to my podcast needs and refreshing options based on the time of day. During my walks, my health and audio apps are ready to tap, sitting conveniently on top of the search menu. Closer to bedtime when I'm ready to unwind, my social media apps are displayed predominantly. I'm having to do fewer and fewer clicks to step into my desired digital space.

As technology continues to evolve intelligently, it's important we learn as a species how to use it to our advantage: to propel growth and economic opportunity, not fuel anger and mistrust. When navigating this increasingly digital space, we're urging you to do so actively and with an open mind, as we have tried to do. There is room to think critically in this space without offending or disrespecting the many constituents that Facebook affects today. These constituents include:

Those working in advertising agencies, the media practitioners of the field. Coming from this background ourselves, we are expected to understand the inner dynamics of the advertising world and know where and how our client's advertising dollars flow. It's imperative we take responsibility when we invest on a platform like Facebook because we are choosing to support an organization that's continued to prove it can't be trusted. Agencies should have a clear point of view on where we go from here, but the way in which the traditional agency has functioned in the past no longer serves the environment we are in today. The world of media mark-ups and rate efficiencies are long gone, and brands look to agencies to provide unbiased, unwavering consultancy. Agencies are well-positioned to think critically, ask the right questions, and consult their clients in deeper, more meaningful ways. As practitioners, how can we engage in more genuine and open dialogue at industry events? And how can we begin to encourage a healthy and productive discussion around the many alternatives to Facebook?

In 2020, a civil rights coalition which included the Anti-Defamation League (ADL) and the NAACP, launched the #StopHateforProfit campaign, calling on major corporates to put a pause on advertising on Facebook. They cited the company's "repeated failures to meaningfully address the vast proliferation of hate on its platforms." Starbucks, Facebook's sixth-largest advertiser at that time as well as major outdoor retail brands like Patagonia and The North Face joined the movement. Brands play a critical role in this ecosystem because their dollars are the backbone of the advertising model under which the industry continues to largely operate. Like any other corporate investment, companies need to ensure marketing dollars are being spent on platforms that are in alignment with their own values. In a way, we can encourage the industry to move towards a more conscientious way of marketing.

Through the pandemic, we learnt that consumers hold a vast amount of power. If consumers believe that a brand is unethical or doesn't align with their values, they simply choose not to buy it. We are no longer bound by scarce options, in which we pay servitude to brands out of desperation. There has never been a better time to be a consumer. We should be asking organizations to put their invested capital towards addressing pervasive and large-scale global issues. Generating economic opportunity remains the single best way to tackle many widespread problems. Our opinions of Elon Musk aside, Tesla has arguably done more to tackle climate change more than any isolated environmental activist movement. Brands can and should affect change.

At the same time, there is room for social media companies to diversify their business models out of what's currently an over-reliance on advertising dollars. There is an opportunity to explore subscription revenue streams, as has been suggested for high-followership platforms like Twitter. This requires a fundamental shift in the bedrock of the way social media companies born out of Silicon Valley have operated for a long time. It certainly won't be easy, but it's an alternative worth exploring as it allows for flexibility outside of pure ad dollars.

In the end, the plea to Big Tech companies is a simple one: we live in a society powered by you. We are in constant engagement with your smartphones, tablets, laptops, software as services and other internet-based technologies. We urge you to make time spent on your platforms meaningful and valuable. As future generations continue to spend more time online, that experience needs to be protected and safe. We're changing the way we work and play, and this will present an enormous opportunity for companies to facilitate this change in helpful ways.

News and fact-based journalism have never been more important. To journalists and truth-seekers, keep unearthing stories. Good quality news and our ability to make sense of the world around us in the most unbiased way possible is the only way to steer us out of the polarized mess we find ourselves in. If people, young and old, are increasingly turning to social media for news, shouldn't there be some semblance of protection to ensure content is fact-based and representative of the truth? Governments will have a large role to play in revaluating the rules and regulations for our new digital world order. What's clear is that antiquated legislation won't solve these unique problems.

Lastly, throughout this book we also offer an optimistic view of where we go from here, thrust into the next evolutionary phase of the Internet. Take it or leave it – but we don't believe humanity was ever meant to blossom behind a screen. We were never meant to create boundaries of hate and misunderstanding and depression and anxiety. We were meant to connect and thrive and communicate. And in the words of Scott Galloway, we will embark on this next journey of the Internet with 'no mercy, no malice,' with an intention to shape and build the next phase of the Internet in a way that serves us well.

Our history in the advertising industry is long and winding, but it's brought us to a place of deep appreciation for the space and for its people. To understand how we got here, we need to first go back to the beginning, where it all began for us – to India and Pakistan.

Chapter 1: Culture Crisis
Amina Qureshi
Dona Varghese

"We don't see things as they are, we see them as we are."
- Anaïs Nin

Surprisingly, having lived in over 10 countries – from Indonesia, Malaysia and the United Arab Emirates to the U.S, France and Canada, I've had a deep-seated appreciation for how different cultures and societies perceive, adopt and use social platforms. It's worth noting that none of these countries are my country of origin as I was born in Pakistan, truly making me a Third Culture Kid (TCK).

Identity was always a difficult thing for me to come to terms with. While my parents reinforced a strict Pakistani identity, having never lived there, I didn't *feel* Pakistani. I felt Western, more like my peers growing up in America or Europe. It was difficult because I had constant pressure at home to be more traditional, whereas anybody who knows me now, will attest to the fact that I am anything but traditional. The pressure to conform to a culture I identified very little with unintentionally made me rebel against it even more – against the culture, against the way things were done in Pakistan, against religion and against my parents.

Through the years, I aptly learned how to wear very different hats depending on whom I was around and whom I needed to impress. Incidentally, the more hats I wore, the less I knew or understood the person inside me. My true self was suppressed and suffocated until I was nothing but a shell of a human in a desperate state to conform. My opportunity finally came when I left for university. I graduated high school with distinguished honors as salutatorian and attended the University of British Columbia. There, I would study Jungian psychology and ancient religions, Renaissance art history and the history of sexuality. This was where I belonged. I have always prided myself on being intellectual and highly educated. I was now amongst other peers from all over the world who were equally motivated to succeed and have some fun along the way. I developed a deep-seated respect for medicinal hallucinogens, for Bob Dylan and for the great Pacific Northwest. I also took one course that left an indelible impression on me for years to come and that course was Cultural Psychology 101.

It was the first time I learned about Third Culture Kids (TCKs) in an academic setting. It turns out there's a very real phenomena for what I went through and felt. TCK's are defined as "individuals who are raised in a culture other than their parents' or the culture of their country of nationality, and also live in a different environment during a significant part of their child development years." Being born in Pakistan, we would visit it frequently, but I had never lived there. In a way, I was always an outsider looking in, thus giving me a unique understanding and perspective of what was going on around me culturally. Never truly identifying with any one culture, but a chameleon in perpetual adaptive mode.

The population of Pakistan is 216,000,000, which is almost six times the population of Canada, where I live today. The dense community coupled with unbridled poverty proliferate barriers to technological adoption. Technological adoption is important for the growth of societies because it's a key component of economic advancement. Technological progress allows for the more efficient production of more and better goods and services – the fundamental cornerstone of success for a capitalistic economy.

On those brief trips back to Pakistan, I was amazed by the sluggishness of social media adoption. I was among the cohort that was exposed to Facebook when it was still only permitted to university students in North America. In fact, I had to use my university email address to sign up for an account. I signed up in the early 2000s, as I began my undergraduate degree at UBC.

The platform instigated excitement among first-year students because it granted an almost secret window into the lives of our dorm room peers. I had other students adding me as a friend even before I arrived for my first day at UBC! In a strange, almost surreal way, it felt as though I had already solidified a handful of friendships before even physically arriving. And the more friends I added, the more comfortable I felt about my first day there. And this, of course, is the poisoned seed of what became the central and explosive issue around Facebook – a false sense of community tucked away inconspicuously behind a screen.

These loose Facebook friendships began to form the basis for social anxiety and ambiguous social norms. Walking to and from class, I would regularly make eye contact with someone I was connected to on Facebook but had never met in person. There was an awkward understanding that we had both likely dug through the troves of each other's social profiles but hesitated to say 'hi' in real life. Our initial eye contact would morph into an awkward half-smile and then immediately we would pass each other without any further interaction. These uncomfortable encounters would happen on the way to class, at university parties, in the library, at campus restaurants and virtually everywhere else that was publicly accessible. But despite feeling a sense of ambiguity around how to appropriately deal with these situations, I would continue to obsessively accept any Facebook invitation as a continued, silent nod to my increasing acceptance and popularity at school.

Understandably, when I would visit Pakistan during winter or summer breaks, I was astonished that my cousins had no knowledge of Facebook. To communicate, they were still SMSing one another on Nokia phones. Their network sphere was limited, because SMS meant having somebody's phone number and realistically, you could only obtain phone numbers of your close friends or family members. Simultaneously, they were perplexed at why I would intentionally opt to connect with strangers. It was a strange thing to try to explain.

This dichotomy in adoption is of course today explained through rigorous psychological and cultural discourse. Technological adoption is slowed by economic hardships, limited access to education and vast poverty – but there's another element at play. One of the most important dimensions of culture is individualism vs. collectivism. In fact, cross-cultural psychology theories and empirical research suggest that culture impacts everything from attitudes to motivations to needs, as well as responses toward social media. Based on the dimensions of individualism vs. collectivism, the way in which people across the world use social media sites as a means of communicating or exchanging information differs greatly.

What exactly characterizes individualism vs. collectivism? We've likely all felt the outputs of these ideologies, but they're so firmly ingrained in our beliefs, behaviours, values, and morals that we've been affected by them without our implicit realization. An individualist is motivated by personal rewards and benefits. They set personal goals and objectives based on a notion of the 'self' and they are comfortable working autonomously, as opposed to within a team. A collectivist is motivated by group goals, they value long-term relationships, and they easily sacrifice individual benefit or praise to recognize and honour their team's success. In fact, being singled out and honoured as an individual from the rest of the team may be perceived as embarrassing to the collectivistic person. Blowing these characteristics out from the individual to the culture at large, the generalized geographic clusters of individualism may be found in Anglo countries, Germanic Europe, and Nordic Europe. Geographic clusters for collectivism are often located in Arab countries, Latin America, Southern Asia, and Sub-Saharan Africa.

Interestingly, individualism vs. collectivism also affects the way people in different countries perceive and use social media. People in East Asian countries like China were found to be more restrained on social media and posted less information about themselves, as Chinese culture values modesty over self-promotion. In individualistic cultures like the United States, contrastingly, social media serves as an important platform for self-expression and self-realization.

There are two additional dimensions that shape and affect the way we understand the world around us: power distance and uncertainty avoidance. Geert Hofstede, a social psychologist best known for his pioneering research on cross-cultural groups and organizations, defines 'power distance' as "the extent to which the members of a society accept that power in institutions and organizations is distributed unequally." Cultures differ in their level of power distance, and those with high power distance justify inequalities in the society or ingroup, whereas those with low power distance are more concerned with maintaining equality. Countries with high power distance include Malaysia, Philippines, Mexico, and China, among others, whereas Austria, Israel, Denmark, and New Zealand have low power distance.

The second dimension – uncertainty avoidance – is anecdotally illustrated in what I discussed earlier in this chapter: the anxiety felt from not knowing how to behave in ambiguous situations. In my example, the uncertainty I experienced when the connections I made on Facebook were superficial, and a real-life connection was non-existent. Uncertainty avoidance deals with a society's tolerance for uncertainty and ambiguity. It indicates to what extent a culture programs its members to feel either comfortable or uncomfortable in unstructured situations.

Unstructured situations are characterized as novel, unknown, surprising, and different from usual. Uncertainty avoidance cultures try to minimize the possibility of such situations with strict laws and rules, safety, and security measures.

Perhaps such fundamental differences in the way we perceive and use social media explains why it's such a difficult topic to understand politically. We can't enact over-arching governance or laws around it because it's so fundamentally different across countries and regions. Culturally, our understanding and beliefs around social media vary and therefore, the laws that govern us around it differ too.

In university, I didn't purport to have any real answers on how to live my life. I completed a thesis on early therapeutic trials of hallucinogenic substances in the 1960s and increasingly became convinced that most constructs were a by-product of culture. Your environment matters. The people you spend your time with matter. The beliefs you hold to be true matter. The story you tell yourself matters.

And it was at that point that I vowed to re-write my story. I couldn't end it as a lost, confused third culture kid. I finally put in the effort to understand myself. Through yoga, a disciplined understanding and practice of meditation, and an obsessive desire to be the best version of myself, I began shedding the identities and cloaks that no longer served me.

I graduated, entered the advertising industry, worked to gain roles of increasing importance, managed high-performing teams, began teaching, had a kid, began working in tech and wrote a book. To those who question if the obstacle is the way, I'm here to tell you it is. Your mindset will determine whether you live a happy and fulfilled life or whether you will suffer in silence. Open your mind, dissolve your ego, and your opportunities will be boundless.

— *Amina Qureshi*

I was born in Dubai, United Arab Emirates and spent most of my adolescent life shuttling between India and the Middle East – between my parents and boarding school. As a third culture kid, I consider myself to be the perfect example of all the trauma a third culture kid experiences, yet I find a sense of comfort in a deep state of limbo.

Growing up in India, I felt out of place. When I went back to Dubai to visit my parents, I also felt out of place. Even today, after spending over three decades in different parts of the world – if someone asks me where I am from, I'm always tempted to say, "I'm not really sure". I wouldn't have it any other way though. I consider it a true privilege to have moved and lived in different parts of India, South Africa, the Middle East, and America. I'm lucky to have been able to build a great support system, and find love and abundance in every place I have lived in.

Even though I have lived in many houses there is only one home for me, really. My home is where my family is and my sense of home is not bound by any place or thing. I like to consider myself a nomad; every couple of years I pack up my bags and set up a life in a new place and live like a local. A decade ago when I was in Pretoria, South Africa, having access to internet was optional outside of one's place of work. I worked for a technology company, and after I left work my life involved time away from screens!

Today, we live in a world where topics around Digital Detox or listening to podcasts on how to free our minds are common. In the late 90s, when I was in boarding school in Kochi, Kerala, screen time was scheduled on weekends or with special permission. We used to go to the school library to check out books for entertainment, deep learning and to work on assignments. Today, these options are just a mere second away, and we have AI platforms to create content for us. In a conversation with a baby boomer the other day (people born between 1945 - 1964), I realized that technological advancements shot up exponentially over the last 2 decades – whether it's the evolution of the internet, the explosion of communication mediums, advertising and data or mobile phones, just to name a few. Today, the digital playground is vast, accessible, and lush with opportunities offering every participant an even playing field. Everyone has a unique and compelling story about their relationship with technology and how it has impacted their lives, for the good or bad.

In the early 2000s when I began thinking about my career, I realized how the impact of cultural diversity and my unique experience in tech consumption would enable me to pursue a fulfilling career in marketing.

I mastered the marketing field, working for some of the biggest companies in the industry. Ultimately, I started my own company called DV Media Co. – and I built it like a nomadic circus. DV Media Co. sets up shop wherever our resources are required: we perform, we entertain, we cash in, and we move on. This is where my boarding school experiences and impact of being a third culture kid kicked in – to be flexible, adaptive and thrive in different cultures with ease.

In the grand scheme of things, how does cultural diversity impact tech usage and understanding? How is culture impacting our consumption habits? Marketing and technology are a cultural phenomenon and are deeply influenced by the culture and conditioning that society is exposed to. There's a documentary called Coded Bias that explores the fallout of MIT Media Lab researcher Joy Buolamwini's discovery that facial recognition does not see dark-skinned faces accurately, and her journey to push for first-ever legislation in the U.S. to govern against bias in the algorithms that impact us all. How often are you pausing to think about YOUR relationship with technology and the tools that enable your digital and technological infrastructure? For most of us, it's something we mostly take for granted. We barely notice it.

I'm currently residing in India, my home country as per my passport – a country with one of the largest democracies and population (both on ground AND online). It's predicted that by 2025, India will have 900 million active internet users. I often wonder – what's the impact of having so many active internet users and having data collected at such a large scale? Do we still have free will or are algorithms determining our day to day lives? If tech platforms are being held responsible for creating bias in politics, what is the political economy of communications in India today? The line between what's real and what's imagined is getting blurrier as sobriety on the matter sets in.

Today, India has over 750 million users. In a country with such a large internet population, one must also ask how did Covid-19 impact her digital evolution?

Amid the coronavirus pandemic, we were all desperate for information. We wanted to know where the virus came from, whether there's a cure, how to stay safe, and of course, we are all wondering when life will once again obtain the quality of normality.

In the case of Covid-19, information can be a literal life-saver – when it's true. Wrong information doesn't help anyone and can obviously make things worse. And like a virus, wrong information can spread, causing what's become known as an infodemic. 2020 was truly the year of false and misleading information. Misinformation is "false information that is spread, regardless of intent to mislead." The spread of misinformation happens often in our everyday lives. We human beings – news flash – are not perfect. We all make mistakes. We all forget things. We mishear or misremember details. We tell our friends something we heard on TV or saw on social media that wasn't true. If you are echoing information that is wrong, but you don't know that it's wrong – I hate to break it to you, but you're still, technically, spreading misinformation.

Disinformation means "false information, as about a country's military strength or plans, disseminated by a government or intelligence agency in a hostile act of tactical political subversion." The term is also used more generally to mean "deliberately misleading or biased information; manipulated narrative or facts; propaganda."

So, disinformation is knowingly spreading misinformation. Our first definition of this word gives one major reason why a person or group might want to spread "fake news", but there are many other nefarious motivations lurking behind the creation of disinformation.

According to Niranjan Sahoo, a political author, "Since the late nineteenth century, the primary source of political and societal polarization in India has been a fundamental question of nationhood: Should India be a secular country or a Hindu Rashtra (Hindu Nation), given that roughly 80 percent of the population is Hindu? Changes in the media landscape have contributed to the problem of polarization, misinformation, and disinformation.

Particularly since the landslide electoral victories of the Hindu nationalist Bharatiya Janata Party (BJP) in 2014 and 2019, the consequences of severe polarization have grown ever more worrisome. Partisan attacks on India's independent political institutions have intensified, opposition parties have become extremely wary of defending pluralism and secularism, and hatred and violence against minority communities have flared up. The coronavirus pandemic has eased this polarization on the surface by engendering more unifying political leadership, yet at the societal level, the crisis has only amplified intolerance, particularly against India's Muslim minority community. Although various actors have launched efforts to counter   the country's majoritarian turn and improve civic dialogue, polarization   in India is more toxic today than it has been in decades, and it shows no signs of abating. Since 2014, Modi's polarizing leadership and the BJP's stunning electoral success under his watch have escalated tensions dramatically."

Covid-19 brought a sense of solidarity through a sense of suffering – but does standing out on our private balconies, lighting candles, and practicing yoga eliminate the complex ramifications of a politically polarized population? A trending hashtag on Twitter in 2020 was CoronaJihad – the latest manifestation of islamophobia. Even though Prime Minister Narendra Modi promotes solidarity and self-reliance, suffering doesn't choose its recipients by religion, caste, or creed. It didn't stop Social Media platforms and WhatsApp groups from being flooded by calls for social and economic boycotts of Muslims, nor did it stop numerous physical attacks on Muslims, including volunteers distributing relief material, amid falsehoods accusing them of spreading the virus deliberately. It was a war of information!

India is a mobile-first digital economy – her call to action for most things is via QR code. It's a great starting point to connect offline media to online media. Let's be real, India's online population's potential is exponential. Everyone wants a piece of India's internet population pie. Ignorant to whether politicians will use this reach to promote polarization, whether brands will create unattainable desire and consumerism, whether FOMO (Fear of Missing Out) will lead to anxiety, panic attacks and depression. The impact on the online population when algorithms are written for advertisers' benefits… well, it's kind of immeasurable.

India's large internet population is a playground filled with bullies who spew hate speech, polarization of thought and actions, insatiable consumerism and fanaticism – just like the rest of the world. It isn't all bad news though. According to Oxford Economics, YouTube's creative ecosystem contributed $88 Million to the economy of India in 2020 and #CreatingForIndia. India's affordable connectivity has improved education, employment opportunities and access to financial services and healthcare information. Covid-19 accelerated the digital evolution in India, no doubt. We must understand the fact that internet awareness and digital skills are intrinsically linked. In India, tech companies like Google, Tinder and Bumble launch TVCs (Television Commercials) to educate the masses about how to use these products. The good is as good as the bad is bad.

In India, Twitter differentiates itself from other social media networks, in that it plays an important role in journalism. The medium on Twitter is conversation, and conversation evolves. Ideally it evolves in a way that we all learn from, but that isn't always the case. Twitter has this sense of fluidity that real journalists and real intellectuals rely on to have conversation. TV news use Twitter to leverage their stories. Twitter is not a Social Network – it is an Interest-based Network, simply talking about a topic puts one on Twitter. It's great for investigative journalism. It's a marketplace of ideas.

Other social platforms encourage community building. Facebook is like your online scrapbook – it has your details, some pictures, your likes and dislikes and you connect with mostly people you know. Meanwhile, Instagram is your medium for personal branding and publicizing your private life in filtered versions of all key moments. It's also become a powerful business platform where a new business model was born – Direct to Customer.

Each social network plays a different role and has the reach to start movements. From an Interest-based Network point of view let's take a moment to look at top users on Twitter by followers. These people have the reach to start a conversation and observe the evolution of this conversation.

Top 50 Twitter users by followers			
#	Profile	Followers	Following	Tweets
1	Barack Obama	108,889,062	586,226	16,407
2	Justin Bieber	105,485,635	284,983	31,415
3	Katy Perry	108,889,062	236	11,569
4	Rihanna	105,485,635	997	10,620
5	Cristiano Ronaldo	98,197,250	60	3,770
6	Taylor Swift	90,338,646	0	716
7	Lady Gaga	84,390,721	118,367	9,734
8	Elon Musk	77,648,525	113	17,114
9	Ellen DeGeneres	77,619,606	26,418	23,704
10	Narendra Modi	76,828,322	2,430	32,236

(Source: Socialtracker // Updated March 14, 2022)

The top 10 list includes Politicians, Musicians, Actors, Footballers and Techo King (Elon Musk's unofficial nickname). This list shows us that Barack Obama was a popular American President and is going down in history for more reasons than his Twitter stats. Another American President, Donald Trump's (before Twitter permanently banned Trump from the platform in January 2021 during the final days of his term) handle @realDonaldTrump had over 88.9 million followers, which would make him number 7 on this list.

Indian Prime Minister Narendra Modi is number 10! As a keen observer of his digital impact, we can see his online image was constructed and evolved over time. His presence exceeds 32,236 Tweets over a span of 13 years, and he's been Prime Minister since 2014. These individuals have the reach to influence millions of people worldwide with just 280 characters.

The real question here is how do politicians use Twitter, and does it matter? The adoption of social media as tools for political communication is expected to generate new forms of communication between politicians and their electorate – provoking more dialogical forms of communication and allowing politicians to personally talk to their followers.

The internet and social media platforms, most significantly Twitter and Facebook, have brought with them an apparent opportunity to transform the way citizens and politicians communicate with one another. Their rise to prominence could have the potential to end the old 'top-down' model of political communication and help close our democratic deficit. But are our political leaders up to the challenge?

While the new media model of political communication has the potential to allow for increased dialogue between political representatives and the public and the opportunity to sculpt a more communicative and involving democracy, we're not quite there yet.

A quick assessment of prominent political actors' use of social media suggests that politicians primarily use communication tools as instruments of broadcast, and not generally in ways that could create a more engaging political communications environment.

Yes, it's apparent that social media is a key medium through which we communicate with each other: it is at the centre of the very structures of our daily interactions. Yet this infiltration is not unique to interpersonal relations. Political leaders, governments, and states operate within this social media environment, wherein they continually address crises and institute damage control through platforms such as Twitter. A question arises here as to what the turn to Twitter means for conventional structures of power and different levels of communication.

There is a deep tendency of people identifying as party supporters to view opposing partisans negatively and co-partisans positively. Affective polarization has become a defining feature of twenty-first-century politics, but we do not know how it relates to citizens' policy opinions.

Answering these questions has fundamental implications not only for understanding the political consequences of polarization, but also for understanding how citizens form preferences. Under most political circumstances, this is a difficult question to answer, but the novel coronavirus pandemic allows us to understand how partisan animus contributes to opinion formation.

In the information era where people are always connected, mindless consumption is king. People don't want to have real conversations anymore because it takes place in real-time, and they can't control what they are going to say. Texting, email and posting allows us to be the selves we want to be. We get to edit but that means we get to delete; we get to retouch. Human relationships are messy, so we clean them up with technology; we sacrifice conversation for connection. It's so easy to have a Facebook page, Twitter feed and acquire many automatic listeners. The illusion of companionship without the demands of friendship. How did we get from connection to isolation? What if there was a way to measure the health of a conversation? There is a lot of conversation around mental health in the digital space. We try to optimize every interstitial moment of our lives; we feel guilty if we are not making every moment count. Even though we are connected and highly functional human beings, we are also highly vulnerable to advancement in technology.

If we go back to the roots, Network Science is an academic field, which studies complex networks such as telecommunication, computer, biological, cognitive, semantic, and social networks -- considering distinct elements or actors. From that point of view, if we look at social networks (the ones we engage in) and hierarchies' networks (the ones we inhabit in), history tends to be written by hierarchical networks. History of public life led to the print evolution and now the history of private life has led to social media evolution. What took a century in the 16th century takes a decade in the 21st century.

When Silicon Valley started the social media evolution, they thought everybody being connected would solve all problems. Since, there has been tremendous change in the public sphere. Networks monetize on high user engagement rates. Would there even be a President Trump without Facebook? The ugly truth is that people are attracted to fake, they are attracted to extremes. And technological advancements and social media have polarized the world in every sense; there seems to be no middle ground.

Today, we experience an omnipresent awareness of the world, and this has a deep impact on our brains. We live in a reality of hyper-personalized news feeds, where no two individuals are consuming the same information – information that confirms our beliefs and makes us feel accepted, or information that challenges our belief system and makes us feel alone and helpless. Simply put, technological advancement doesn't match our evolutionary advancement – leading to issues like misinformation, disinformation, affective polarization, deepfake, depression, anxiety, the list goes on. In fact, technological advancement is directly proportional to the downgrading of humanity.

If we are what we consume, then what do your consumption habits say about you? When I decided to make a living out of consumerism, I became highly conscious about my consumption habits. Perhaps it's an occupational hazard or I'm just like a drug dealer – someone who sells more and rarely consumes. Whatever the case may be, I set some ground rules for my sanity and success. I value deep focus and concentration and in the quest for such, I've managed to set healthy boundaries with the impact technology has on my mental health and making sense of the world around us. I do not compromise on my me-time – I visit my mind palace very often (at least once a day), I practice Yin Yoga, a form of yoga which encourages stillness and I clock in at least 7 hours of sleep. No matter where I am in the world, this way of life goes with me.

— *Dona Varghese*

Chapter 2: Pulling the Strings
Amina Qureshi

"It's not a question of enough, pal. It's a zero-sum game: somebody wins, somebody loses. Money itself isn't lost or made, it's simply transferred from one perception to another."
- Gordon Gekko, Wall Street

Back in the early 2000s, I had just entered the media industry – bright eyed and ready to make an impact. I had worked in marketing for many years prior – with a stint on the social media side of things at a traditional public relations firm in Montreal, then transitioned over to content marketing in Dubai. Blessed with a blissful naivety back then, transitioning into advertising meant that I had finally made it. I would be handling clients with big budgets and, with that, would come greater responsibility and decision-making powers.

The media agency world was fragmented then. Nebulous display advertising was still a regular part of every media mix. Programmatic media was in its infancy and agencies were beginning to realize the commercial impact of bundled services and non-transparent media practices. It was a lucrative game to be a part of. Digital advertising promised an entirely new revenue stream in advertising, and nobody truly yet knew how it worked.

It's safe to say, when I began my career in advertising, there was no real "problem." Sure, we engaged in ambiguous practices under the guise of bundled programmatic departments or perhaps bought questionable media placements because we were taken out for overpriced cocktails – but there was never any issue. We chalked it up to working in a fun industry with great perks. It was a whirlwind of fun back then. Every day at 4 pm we would look to wrap up early and head to the local advertising industry watering hole at Radisson Blu on the outskirts of Dubai Media City. As day turned to night, we would blissfully drink martinis with our industry peers, basking in riding shotgun on this new ad-tech wave.

Simply said, the agency world – particularly in Dubai – was the place to be in late 2012. Google and Facebook were growing, but there was still generous room for other ad-tech players and their sales teams. The smaller digital vendors like InMobi or AdZouk had deep pockets for networking, which they would dip into regularly to make sure we were happy, satisfied clients. We had great partnerships with them, and they would regularly work with us to help win pitches and bring on new business.

In 2015, when we received an RFP to pitch for the regional Coca-Cola business at MediaCom, I immediately and ambitiously raised my hand to be the digital lead on the pitch. I had never led a pitch before, let alone for one of the world's biggest brands. The experience could be summed up as insurmountable panic and dread, later followed by excitement and resourcefulness. I've always had a knack for figuring things out and so I got to work. We pulled in global MediaCom resources from London and flew them to Dubai for two weeks to assist in the process.

There was a woman named TJ Lightwala, an industry agency veteran back then. She headed up the digital discipline at Mindshare Dubai and was well-connected with the teams across GroupM. She was assigned to help me craft the pitch and I was thrilled to be able to learn from one of the best. I was young, motivated, and smart enough to figure it out. I recall being in awe of the way she understood marketing and strategy – during our brainstorming sessions, she would adeptly talk about market dynamics, how to steal competitive share, and which types of segments to pursue. It was impressive.

She was also the first woman I watched command dominance in a room filled with men. Advertising had notoriously always been a male-dominated industry, but particularly so in the Middle East. Female voices were regularly drowned out or unheard, so when TJ came into the fold – it was refreshing to see a bold and steadfast woman running the show. Without me even realizing what was happening, she taught me the discipline, rigor and boldness required to succeed in advertising.

The days crept by and we inched closer to pitch day. The night before the pitch, we were amid what seemed like the fiftieth dry run. If I displayed a flicker of uncertainty or wavered in my confidence to deliver, we would start all over again. Each time refining, each time iterating, each time perfecting. It was the first seed planted in my professional DNA to strive for excellence, but favour progress over perfection. At some point, our CEO at the time shut down the dry runs. He realized we would need to sleep and eat to deliver well, too.

The next day was pitch day. I quelled my nerves and delivered with hawk precision, clarity and excellence. We went out for celebratory drinks afterward and I was showered with praise. That night, I went home confident that we would win the business. A few weeks later, we received an email from the Coca-Cola client leading the pitch. It was a difficult decision, they said, but they chose to proceed with another agency. It was a punch to the gut. How could I have been so confident that we would win this and failed to deliver?

It was only later that news surfaced of which agency had won the pitch. It was a competitor agency, and Coca-Cola had chosen to go with them for one, primary reason: this agency could attain more efficient buying rates on digital platforms like Facebook and Twitter. They didn't have the stronger pitch and they didn't have a more visionary prospect for the future of Coca-Cola in the Middle East. They promised more media space for less. This was the first time I understood that advertising was fundamentally still a business, and efficiencies still mattered.

Social media was still relatively new. There were only a handful of advertising options available on Facebook and Twitter, and we were certainly working within a very primitive world of data-driven marketing. In short, there were not yet enough users passing enough data to the platforms for there to be any real concern over data or privacy. These companies were still in the throes of understanding their own commercial model based on the basic tenets of supply and demand. They understood that if they had a limited amount of inventory available for advertising, they could introduce an auction or bidding environment to drum up buying prices.

Today, Google and Facebook's market share of digital advertising revenues is 80% – up from 66% just a mere five years ago. And you might be asking yourself, so what? Why does it matter if two companies centrally control so much of the Internet? They're providing utility, connectivity, and economic prosperity for a significant portion of the globalized world. So, what's the problem?

The Trade Desk's CEO, Jeff Green, summarizes it best: competition in advertising is necessary to preserve a democratic and Open Internet. One that serves the needs of users, a transparent and accessible Internet that doesn't rely on controlling all ends of the supply chain. The problem with centralized control over data is that these environments become Walled Gardens with little to no oversight into what goes on inside. As Facebook grew its user base and amassed rich troves of data, they increasingly made headlines for being on the wrong side of privacy.

Like any complex issue, I wanted to understand Facebook's impact on both ends of the spectrum. What made it so unique in its ability to connect the world, and simultaneously so dangerous as a political weapon? Technologists at Facebook argue that technology itself is innocuous. That the intrinsic existence of Facebook is benevolent: it's helped reconnect families across borders, it's enabled an instantaneous flow of information, it's helped overcome mass wastage and irrelevancy in advertising. In fact, it's created an environment where relevancy is the new digital currency. Is it simply a story of a handful of Silicon Valley executives decisioning on the lives of 3 billion individuals for the inherent advancement and good of society? Or is there perhaps something more ominous at play? Are the hyper-personalization algorithms and the fundamental business models of advertising that fuel the system inherently problematic?

In 2021, Facebook's negligence facilitated the genocide of Rohingya Muslims in Myanmar after the social media network's algorithms amplified hate speech and the platform failed to take down inflammatory posts, according to legal action launched in the US and the UK. The platform faces compensation claims worth more than £150bn.

A class action complaint lodged with the northern district court in San Francisco says Facebook was "willing to trade the lives of the Rohingya people for better market penetration in a small country in south-east Asia."

It adds: "In the end, there was so little for Facebook to gain from its continued presence in Burma, and the consequences for the Rohingya people could not have been more dire. Yet, in the face of this knowledge, and possessing the tools to stop it, it simply kept marching forward."

Perhaps the 2016-2017 Russian interference in the U.S. elections will still ring a bell. In fact, there were two separate Russian campaigns on Facebook during the 2016 election. The first came from Russia's military intelligence agency, the GRU. Facebook first discovered GRU activity in March 2016, according to a post-mortem circulated internally the following year. GRU agents made fake Facebook accounts and pages and used them to spread disinformation and false news. Alex Stamos, former chief security officer of Facebook, reported on what his team found with the FBI, alerting both CEO Mark Zuckerberg and COO, Sheryl Sandberg. Both executives chose to turn a blind eye to the information brought forward.

Facebook was slow to remove some of what it found, in part because at the time it had no rule against foreign entities setting up groups and pages to manipulate American opinion. After Facebook became aware that a Russian-operated page known as DCLeaks was distributing stolen emails from the Clinton campaign to journalists on the platform, the company initially took no action. Only after a security analyst found that the documents contained personal information — a clear violation of Facebook rules — was DCLeaks eventually banned.

But even as the company investigated, it said nothing publicly.

Within the threat intel group, there was debate over what should be done. Facebook was a private company, some argued, not an intelligence agency; the platform was not duty-bound to report its findings. For all Facebook knew, the National Security Agency was tracking the same Russian accounts the company was seeing, and possibly planning arrests. It might be irresponsible for Facebook to say anything. Others argued that Facebook's silence was facilitating Russian efforts to spread the stolen information. They said the company needed to make public that Russia-linked accounts were spreading hacked documents through Facebook. To them, the situation felt like a potential national emergency. "It was crazy. They didn't have a protocol in place, and so they didn't want us to take action. It made no sense," one security team member said. "It felt like this was maybe a time to break precedent."

While these incidents continued to make headlines around the world, I continued to feel uncomfortable assigning dollars to Facebook on any media plan. In 2016, I was handling advertising for McDonald's, one of the world's largest advertisers. We spent millions of dollars with Facebook. It was at this point, that I began to publicly voice my opposition towards the platform, however, we were still held to investing with them because it was profitable for the agency. Looking back, I often ask myself, when did I reach this tipping point? At what point did Facebook enact one too many aggressions? We seem to have reached a nexus in time where understanding the effects of Facebook and Instagram are no longer considerations or after-thoughts, but imperatives if we want our species to coexist against increasingly complex technologies and systems.

If we take it from the whistleblowing executives at Google, Facebook, Twitter and Uber who voiced their concerns in *The Social Dilemma*, a 2020 exposé documentary on Netflix, these companies intentionally engineered their platforms to be as addictive as possible. Tristan Harris, formerly a Design Ethicist at Google, is at the forefront of the documentary and details a fascinating and multi-pronged explanation of the issues with technology, the advertising model, and the highly sophisticated, attention-hijacking algorithmic models at play.

Those who don't quite understand what media people do – I tend to describe us as middlemen. We facilitate the buying of media – hundreds of millions of dollars' worth every year. We advise clients on their media strategy and subsequently, where they should be investing their dollars most effectively. Every year, Google, Facebook, Twitter, and other social platforms approach us for annual upfronts. This is industry-speak for an understood agreement on how much investment we will spend with them that year. In return, they give us various, otherwise unattainable opportunities in specialized measurements, innovation ideas, bonus media dollars, numerous lavish dinners and cocktail parties, trips to their motherships in Palo Alto and virtually any other perk.

We continued to invest with Facebook long after stories began breaking about their misuses of customer data. Problems weren't only on the data side of things. Slowly, we began hearing of studies that insinuated Facebook had pervasively negative impacts on happiness and wellbeing levels, particularly among younger females. However, we continued to invest with them as part of our day job. I still bought into Facebook's story that they wanted to "Bring the World Closer Together" by connecting global audiences.

Funnily enough, far from bringing people together, research indicates that human beings can only maintain relationships with a maximum of 150 other individuals. A Facebook user, on average, has 338 'friends'. This poses an interesting conundrum for psychologists, sociologists, behavioral economists, and anybody interested in studying the effects of technology on human behavior. It suggests that we are far from understanding the impact technology has had on 4.5 billion individuals — about 60% of the global population.

If we go back to the beginning, when Facebook launched in February 2004, Mark Zuckerberg seemed more concerned with the usability and friendliness of the platform than with its monetization. He scoffed when his co-founder Eduardo Severin proposed they introduce advertising to offset the increasing costs of servers, a by-product of their vastly growing user base. And for two months, he stood his ground and opposed the advertising model. Turns out, no matter how noble or just the cause for technology may be, there comes a tipping point where mounting costs must be accrued for. And so, in April 2004, the first ads on Facebook appeared. Introducing advertising to cover every day operating costs seemed justified — it rang no alarm bells.

Arguably, Facebook had no early expertise in advertising or monetization. But they had a real firm stronghold on their product and their audience. The first Facebook ads that were permitted had to mold into the platform as seamlessly as possible — as though they were natively integrated. The amount of advertising was limited. Facebook wanted to preserve and honor the user experience and conserve the idea that it was intrinsically a space to connect with your friends and family, without the onslaught of irrelevant and annoying ads. Zuckerberg shunned bigger, more monolithic advertising models from the likes of Goldman Sachs, Mercer Management Consulting, etc. because he felt the platform was powerful enough without an overreliance on ads. Above each advertisement on Facebook, a witty remark stated, "We don't like these either, but they pay the bills."

Facebook wasn't the only one to express skepticism around advertising in its early days. Google-founders Larry Page and Sergey Brin had similar remarks around an advertising model when they launched Google Search. They were vehemently opposed to it and mentioned if the monetization of Search was possible in any other way, they would pursue it. They even admitted that advertising posed a serious conflict of interest within a consumer platform aimed at delivering the most relevant information to a customer's search query. But no other monetization model proved effective enough to keep up with the hyper-growth model of Silicon Valley. They ultimately surrendered to advertising.

The decision to keep ad dollars at bay felt as if Facebook genuinely intended to put its users at the centre of everything it was building. Zuckerberg scoffed at the multi-billion-dollar advertising industry that loomed menacingly above. The initial growth of Facebook was predicated on values and ideologies around expansion, free speech, accessibility, and knowledge sharing. By putting the advertising model on the side-lines, they conveyed to the public that they weren't motivated by revenue and greed. In its early days, it felt like Facebook was offering to propel us into an era of connectedness, happiness and productivity.

And for that brief moment, I believed it.

A decade later, the advertising model had quickly become Facebook's primary revenue driver. If greed wasn't a motivating factor at the start, it certainly seemed to be at the centre of decision-making for future growth. The problem with large-scale global problems is that nobody sees them coming; there's no precedence. When Mark Zuckerberg created Facebook, there was no precedent for large-scale data misuse, online addiction, teen bullying, fake news, and the whole slew of concerns later brought about by the platform.

But just when the doom and gloom around Facebook seemed pervasive, there appeared a silver lining. And that silver lining just so happened to be the global pandemic. While the world shuttered in from COVID-19, we were finally given the opportunity to take a deep breath and examine what was going on around us. It caused a seismic shift in the way we understood our place in the world and because of that, we had to rethink how marketing could address the ever-changing needs of the customer. Organizations were forced to ask themselves what value or purpose their organization fulfilled. They began to understand what it meant to truly put the customer at the centre. Brands began communicating their 'why'.

The pandemic placed the burden of responsibility on brands to be clear and concise about their positioning and purpose in the marketplace. There is a need and desire for brands to be genuine. At the heart of it, is a desire for transparency. Companies are expected to be transparent in how they operate: from practices and policies to algorithms and code. Only through transparency are we able to foster a new environment in which marketing has a crystal-clear role to play in defining an organization's future relationship with customers – built around trust and confidence.

As we navigate into the next phase of the Internet and try to understand the impact of further digitization in our lives, trust and transparency become even more important. Web3 at times can feel like a black market; some dark unknown marketplace of greed. If brands are expected to evolve their presence in this space, they need credible, trusted environments. If Facebook has shown that it can't honor data and privacy in the material world we currently live in, its ability to do so in the metaverse strikes me as doubtful.

Like every social phenomenon in history, Facebook was not created in a vacuum. It was the by-product of shifting modes of communication, shifting societal values and shifting culture. Whether you're a regular Instagram user, a junior media planner entering the industry or a seasoned veteran questioning the way forward, you must first turn back the pages of history and start at the very beginning. Only when we uncover the mistakes of the past can we develop a true desire to remedy the future.

Chapter 3: Back to the Future
Dona Varghese

"Every challenge you encounter in life is a fork in the road. You have a choice to choose which way to go - backward, forward, breakdown or breakthrough."
- Ifeanyi Enoch Onuoha

In the early 2000s when I began thinking about my career, I knew very little (and had limited access to information) about the different types of career opportunities out there. I had a clear understanding of the strengths I possessed but had no idea how those strengths would translate into any sort of meaningful career. What does it even take to be a marketing professional? What are the traits of a somewhat successful marketer? According to Google Search, good marketing people are first-class communicators, good team players and skilled project managers; with excellent analytic and creative skills. If being a good communicator was essential for a career in marketing, I suddenly knew this was the profession I would pursue. I was ready for the challenging journey ahead.

Marketing is one of the toughest spaces for any type of business and there's a reason it's constantly evolving. Between picking a career trajectory in marketing to pursuing a master's in it, I got to see and experience many moments of evolution. As an industry, we are always in flux, going through changes and implementing them as we go along. So as practitioners, how do we navigate in the age of complex marketing?

A decade ago, when I was in the media planning department for a global tier-one client, most of our investment went towards Yahoo.com, because at the time, they were the best performing platform. Today, Yahoo doesn't even exist in media plans. We are living under the constant fear that our role is going to become redundant. As marketers, we are trained to believe that things are dying, and hence, we are regularly challenging ourselves and others to innovate. At the peak of my career in marketing, I quit my high-paying job in Dubai and moved to New York. I was drawn to the media capital of the world to learn to forecast the future of marketing by looking back into the past. My colleagues thought I was crazy to pack up my everything-is-perfect life in Dubai to study Media Management on the opposite side of the globe.

In late 2016 I got accepted into The New School University, most notably known for their design school – Parsons. I joined The School of Public Engagement. With great ambition, I went back to school to gain a deep academic understanding of this hazy marketing space that is constantly undergoing deaths and rebirths. I also felt a sense of responsibility to study the field I was gaining recognition in – intuitively I felt it was time to ask myself about the impact of the work I was doing and how to do it better.

The New School was started over a century ago by a handful of rebellious professors from Columbia University. These individuals questioned the standard system of education, which was restricted and exclusive. They set out to share knowledge and give people the opportunity to learn what they truly desired to become owners of their own system of education. Dedicated to academic freedom and intellectual inquiry, The New School played a pivotal role in the lives of many over the last century – creating a safe space for progressive thinkers.

With a sense of arrogance and curiosity, I joined The School of Public Engagement after spending a decade in marketing and media. I walked in thinking I would elevate my existing knowledge, but what I learned was that I had to throw that existing knowledge in the trash. Over the course of my master's program, I found myself questioning and challenging the status quo. I got to interact with people from all walks of life, including David Carroll. David is an Associate Professor of Media Design and one of the subjects of Netflix Documentary 'The Great Hack'. Through David, I got deep insight into the world of data. He simply encouraged us to think about where all this data is going. According to David, "the explosion of data is like the problem of piracy – a scourge that affects international spaces, places between jurisdictions where lawlessness thrives – in open waters. Data does not respect borders; it requires effort to monitor and maneuver. And it requires global cooperation. The Cambridge Analytics scandal is a beautiful illustration of the necessity of privacy laws and the way the industry has imposed this data crisis on the world."

Another program that blew my mind and possibly changed my thinking was a course called Media Futures, a 4-month scenario-planning process where we looked back 100 years to forecast the next 100. We divided our analysis into four different scenarios – growth, transformation, constraints, and collapse. Media's business-as-usual addiction to profit spawns social addictions that effectively lobotomize the collective mind (precisely when we need our wits the most). Manoj Fenelon gave us hope and encouraged rejuvenation in the kinds of seeds that certain companies are planting and nurturing.

It is during this class that my vision for the future of media agencies was born – collaborative networks that truly leverage the power of the internet to be a counterforce to consolidation and control, and business models that serve a purpose – rather than the other way around. Working with Manoj Fenelon gave me the confidence I needed to set up my agency. Where purpose and profit can finally intersect. From a theory-based perspective, I urge you to examine Marshall McLuhan's phrase – the medium is the message – and present the argument that changes in modes of communication have a critical impact on the trajectory of social evolution and the values and beliefs of societies.

For McLuhan, it was the medium itself that shaped and controlled "the scale and form of human association and action". Taking social media apps as an example, his theory would imply that the way this medium played with conceptions of speed and time transformed "the world of sharing and connections into the world of creative configuration and digital personas". Therefore, the message of the social media medium is this transition from lineal connections to configurations. McLuhan argues that a "message" is: the change of scale, pace or pattern that an invention or innovation "introduces into human affairs". Social media platforms have changed our way of life. Social "proof" has become an important aspect of success in any space we enter. Social currency is just as important, if not perceptually more important, than financial wealth.

Marshall McLuhan was a visionary, far ahead of his time. This Canadian was a philosopher and professor but could perhaps be best described as a communications theorist. The book is called The Medium is the Massage (Mass-age), due to a mistake made by the typesetters, but when McLuhan saw the error, he loved it and kept it as it was. Perhaps this was because McLuhan thought the media "massage" the brain to behave in particular ways.

So, the medium is the message – what does it mean? Quite simply, it means that the way that we send and receive information is more important than the information itself. When we were once consumers – consuming information by watching television or listening to the radio – in the 21st century we have now also become producers, creating our own information. For instance, after watching the latest episode of a series, we can now instantly connect with anyone anywhere in the world who also watched the same episode and communicate with them. In fact, some tech companies have come out with features that enable people to watch together on the same screen with the option to chat or talk while watching. If a person wants to pause, then everyone on the screen experiences the same feeling when you pause the TV in the den while you go to the toilet. The only difference here is that it's a digital screen experience.

The variety of mediums today have changed the way we behave. Studies have shown that our memory spans have reduced due to digital technology. News stories have been replaced with 280-characters. Conversations have been replaced with emojis. Anecdotally, I've heard of young children trying to turn the volume of their parents arguing down with a remote control. When reading a book, I've had to stop myself from moving my hand to press on a word to get the dictionary definition, after becoming familiar with the tap and look-up user interface. For McLuhan watching television changed the way we looked at the world. He said "It is impossible to understand social and cultural changes without a knowledge of the workings of media." This is developed in the modern world, with social media playing an important part in various civil and cultural events.

Remember the Egyptian revolution of 2011? If it were not for Facebook and other social media networks, the event would not have been nearly as successful of an uprising. Online activism helped to organize and publicize demonstrations and acts of nonviolent civil disobedience, which resulted in the eventual overthrow of the government. McLuhan prophesied that "Electrical information devices for universal, tyrannical womb-to-tomb surveillance are causing a very serious dilemma between our claim to privacy and the community's need to know."

Edward Snowden's whistle-blowing revelations in 2013 exposed the 24/7 global surveillance that intelligence agencies and governments conduct on their citizens. The public opinion of Snowden ranges from hero to traitor and underlines the predicament that affects our society. In McLuhan's world, he refers to "One big gossip column that is unforgiving, unforgetful, and from which there is no redemption." Think about when tweets and comments posted online have resulted in job dismissals, arrests, and online abuse. Deleting them has a minimal impact – anything posted on the internet could theoretically last forever.

Real total war has become a war of information. It is being constantly fought by subtle electric informational media. This has been proven true time and time again, most recently with the 2016 United States Presidential election. The battle for the White House was multifaceted and complex, but information and propaganda were key, with both sides working hard to broadcast their views. The two protagonists, Trump and Clinton, tried to influence the public, with information from WikiLeaks and alleged actions from Russia taking centre stage.

Have you ever thought about the impact of the shifts from oral communication to writing or the shift from print to electronic communication?

What role does hypermedia play in the marketing decisions we make for the brands we represent? And have you thought about how our own understanding impacts the consumers these brands are targeting?

It's argued that different modes of communication have a certain "logic" or "nature" – not in any determinist sense, but of making certain types of communication easier or more difficult. As communication is such a vital part of human existence, a change in the mode of communication will have substantial effects on factors. Impacting the distribution of power within society, the nature and character of individual and social cognition, and the values and beliefs that animate a particular population.

According to legend, Abraham Lincoln was willing to walk several miles to borrow a book while growing up in Indiana during the early nineteenth century. "My best friend is the man who'll get me a book I ain't read," young Lincoln is reported to have said. Literature was scarce, difficult to access, and precious. Not only literature, but information in general was hard to come by. Whether news from afar, new knowledge and insight, or simple entertainment – it usually took effort and considerable expense to get a hold of information.

Flash forward to 2022, where accessing info is no longer the challenge, but navigating through the overload of it is a whole other story. Your typical day in 2022 is no longer a long walk to borrow a book. It's a stroll past face recognition technology, complete with a few distracted taps and clicks. Any search query you make, you have your answers within microseconds. For instance – I opened a new tab, typed in "digital revolutions", and landed on about 50,10,00,000 results in 0.55 seconds. This whole process took less than 10 seconds. A mere 200 years ago we got out of bed, cleaned our teeth, had a meal, changed out of our pyjamas, and planned for the day – all before we even thought about setting out to access information. Today, we don't even have to get out of bed to gather 50,10,00,000 instant results at our fingertips.

Hypermedia's Diana Effect

August 31, 1997, isn't a day I remember every year, but when I do think about the significance of this day, I am always taken back to my seat at the kitchen counter feeling a sense of deep loss. What's etched in my memory is the impact Princess Diana's death had on my mother. She was sincerely and deeply sad – as if she had lost one of her closest friends. My naïve 8-year-old self couldn't help but think how absurd, why is mama crying watching something that happened somewhere else? How can I see and react to what is going on somewhere else, while sitting at home? Today as I examine this moment through an academic and experiential lens, I understand better what my mother and over 2.5 billion people felt as they watched the news of Princess Diana's death. This is what I would file into what people call the Collective Memoir.

Collective Memoir is the power of technology and media to evoke a sense of attachment and nostalgia about things you have nothing to do with. The evolution of social media comes with a sense of collective experience. We are part of things we are not really part of. We are in two places at once, sometimes more, depending on the number of devices in front of you and the number of platforms you have open across each device. In all societies, humans engage in the production and exchange of information, along with symbolic content. Not too long ago, there was a time that communication was linear – a process that didn't include feedback, or it was quite delayed. The linear model was one-way, non- interactive communication. But today's devices can interconnect with each other seamlessly – some at the speed of light. Information flies through the air, bouncing off satellites, and travels across upgraded existing copper wires and cables, through fibre optics. Rather than a single instrument of technology or means of communication, it is this complex, digitally integrated web of communications that defines the hypermedia environment. Now what does this mean for media practitioners? What does it mean for brands? What does this mean for consumers?

In my opinion, the hypermedia environment has enabled Collective Memoir, which in turn increased our levels of empathy – the ability to understand and share the feelings of another. Empathy is an enormous concept. I believe the human race has evolved the way we have because we have the ability to be empathetic. In fact, the Social Media evolution is rooted in our ability to feel empathetic to another's situation. There is always a reason why people are the way they are – and it's our ability to walk in another's shoes that helps us identify those reasons.

Psychologists Daniel Goleman and Paul Ekman have identified three components of empathy:

Cognitive, Emotional and Compassionate.

- Cognitive: Simply knowing how the other person feels and what they might be thinking. Sometimes called perspective-taking.

- Emotional: When you feel the same as the other person, as though their emotions were contagious.
- Compassionate: With this kind of empathy, we not only understand a person's predicament and feel with them, but are spontaneously moved to help, if needed.

On the flipside of empathy, social media platforms have made a lot of headlines in the last decade or so for being on the wrong side of democracy and privacy. Meaning one should think long and hard about how much time we spend on the platforms. For instance, when social media platforms thrive on advertisement models, the users of these platforms are really commodities to facilitate platform growth. And if I draw back to Marshal McLuhan's "the message is the medium"; the effect of the medium is far greater and more vast compared to the message. So, what is the mindset of an individual who is on Discord vs Twitter vs Instagram vs WhatsApp vs Clubhouse vs Netflix vs YouTube? If the same individual is active on all these platforms – does each medium impact the same individual differently? Do these platforms impact the way we live and the way we do things? If prominent mediums set the tone for the society we live in today, are we perhaps highly social, empathetic individuals, seeking instant gratification, objectively or subjectively?

From an ecological and holistic perspective, conceptual, technological, economic, or other changes in human patterns of interactions can alter the human developmental path in unexpected ways that defy more linear notions of changes. TV is stereotypically known as an "idiot box" because as a medium it is subjective, totally involving the audience in ways that prevent them from looking at the message objectively – and when literacy is objective, the subjective medium of the television takes away some of our ability to consume the information it presents without a present bias. If social media is considered not to create hate but rather "gives anyone with a smartphone the ability to broadcast hate speech" while at the same time allowing "connections between individuals that would not otherwise be made." There always seems to be a duality at play here. In 2022, as social media platforms dominate every aspect of our lives – what do we call this era?

We have many instances that shed light on the flip side of social media and empathy, namely Russia's interfering with the 2016 elections, Brexit, Cambridge Analytica and the New Zealand Shooting in March of 2019.

One incident that is very close to my heart is the horrible series of terrorist attacks in Sri Lanka on Sunday, April 21, 2019 – when one of the decisions the government took was to block social media apps. So, what happened?

New York Times reported, "the clock hands on the steeple of St. Anthony's Shrine stuck 8:45 a.m., the exact moment when the first suicide bomber's explosion ripped through wooden pews as Easter Sunday worshipers were praying. Minutes later, a second suicide blast shattered the Sunday brunch tranquility at the Shangri-La Hotel's Table One Restaurant, a favorite among foreign tourists. Within a few hours, suicide bombings hit three Catholic churches and three upscale hotels in the Indian Ocean Island nation of Sri Lanka, still recovering from a quarter-century civil war, in which the suicide bomb was pioneered. The death toll in the attacks rose to 290, with over 500 people wounded. The finance minister, Mangala Samaraweera, called the attacks "a well-coordinated attempt to create murder, mayhem and anarchy."

The bombings were the deadliest attacks on Christians in South Asia in recent history. There has been a rising trend of religious-based violence in the region. The bombings came as Christians and other religious groups have been increasingly targeted in South Asia, where a mix of surging nationalism, faith-based identity politics and social media rumor-mongering has created an atmosphere of combustion. News of the bombings rippled out all Easter morning, interrupting celebrations across the world during a week where Christians were still grieving about the devastating fire at the Norte-Dame cathedral in Paris.

Sri Lanka blocked several social media networks in the wake of the Easter Sunday terrorist attacks, including Facebook and WhatsApp. The extraordinary step reflects growing global concern about the capacity of American-owned networks to spin up violence. Officials blocked the platforms out of fear that misinformation about the attacks and hate speech could spread, provoking more violence. Not surprisingly, a growing body of research has linked social media to religious and racial violence.

Just one of the downfalls of social media as a communication tool is that it's become the means for anyone and everyone to connect and exchange information – including radical groups and individuals. It has integrated into literally everything.

But if we were to analyze the nature of networks, we would conclude that social media platforms build their businesses on sophisticated algorithms that serve up content that keeps users engaged. Favoring posts that tap into negative, primal emotions like anger and fear. When Silicon Valley sparked the social media evolution, they thought connecting humans to one another would solve all problems. The trouble is, there's been tremendous change in the public sphere. Networks monetize on high user engagement rates. And when people are attracted to fake; they are attracted to extremes. We live in a polarized world, and there seems to be no middle ground.

American self-help author Mark Manson says we are what we consume. He says, "When you choose what media to consume, you are choosing your future thoughts and perspectives and opinions. And if you choose poorly, you will think poorly."

As Media Practitioners let's ask ourselves the following questions:

- How have different modes of communication changed the way we live and work?
- What is the role social media plays in journalism?
- What makes a conversation healthy in the digital space?
- What is the nature of networks? Are they good or evil?
- Are media agencies screwed today?

Chapter 4: The Evolution of Agencies
Amina Qureshi

"The greatest danger in times of turbulence is not the turbulence, it is to act with yesterday's logic."
- Peter Drucker

I had moved almost 15 times in my life - packing up and shifting to a different city every 3 years. It had its beauty and its stress. A nomad, shifting from place to place, dreading the inevitable question that comes: "so where's home?" Nowhere and everywhere, I would respond, in a desperate attempt to ignore the question.

After a few years of living in Dubai, I finally got the itch to pack up and move again. I explored Canada and a few cities across the U.S. like Seattle and San Francisco, but nothing felt completely right. Finally, in the summer of 2016, I received an offer to head up advertising for one of the world's most iconic brands – McDonald's. The role was in Toronto, so I gathered my belongings and landed at Pearson Airport. It was a perfectly breezy and sultry summer evening in August. I had lived in Canada before Dubai, so I was accustomed to the country and the culture. Though there is always something unnerving about landing in a brand-new city, this landing was brimming with opportunity and excitement.

My role at McDonald's had a very specific remit: convince owner-operators about the efficacy of their digital ad dollars. McDonald's, for obvious reasons, has always been a traditional-heavy advertiser. Mass reach, mass penetration, low involvement category. For them to continue investing in digital, they demanded to see its impact on same-store sales. Luckily, they'd had a relationship with our agency, Omnicom, for the greater part of the decade, and the ingrained relationship was evident in the deep level of trust they displayed in us.

McDonald's was also a rare account that placed almost equal weight on their creative decisioning as they did on their media decisioning. This was evident in their processes too – they would brief OMD and Cossette, their creative agencies, together. They wanted presentations from both our agencies to be combined into one. If we proposed YouTube, we would have had to have been prepared to present a creative concept. It was a welcomed change from the years prior – in which the media plan dictated the MRF, which dictated the creative units.

There was a lot of ineffective advertising in general back then, and I would argue, even today. Brands, messaging and positioning are all becoming homogeneous. Every brand suggests that it "makes today better" or "inspires creativity for tomorrow" – but these slogans – and by extension, the brands themselves, are mediocre and uninspiring. Marketing professionals today have a burden of responsibility to reinforce proper marketing strategy, derived from experience and expertise. Over time, we've somehow trained marketers to chase after the shiny new thing to the chagrin of tried, true and tested mechanisms for delivering growth. We need to get back to the basics of formulating a clear strategy.

How did we get here? How did we become stuck on a hamster wheel of tactics?

If we go back to the birth of modern advertising, to the 1960s Mad Men heyday, creative was everything. It all started with the brand. What did it stand for? What challenge was it facing in its existing societal context? It was a rich and deep discussion around values and what a brand should stand for. A passionate call for household names to represent something, be purposeful and intentional. Don Draper and his creative department were at the forefront of discussions, while media was a 2-person department, silently shunned to the corner.

This is how it was. Until we realized how to commercialize media – and lots of it. By buying inventory in mass, we were able to secure exceptionally low rates to secure a sizable margin. And this split largely persisted for the next four decades. We saw the split between creative and media agencies and within media agencies, the split between traditional and digital. The end output suffered because of a disconnect between two disciplines that needed to work hand in hand to be effective. The messaging is ultimately useless if it's not placed appropriately, and the placement is ineffective if the message isn't tailored to it. Digital continued to grow right up till 2019: when for the first time, advertisers spent more on digital than they did on traditional.

And that spurred a tipping point.

Companies like Google and Facebook were shaping the marketing conversation. The issue, however, was that this placed unbalanced emphasis on marketing communications – and even within that, digital communications – which equates to only 4% of all marketing. These conversations dismissed other important marketing levers like pricing, distribution, and product. As a result, clients and agencies alike were drawn to the allure of social platforms and as a result, overly focused on tactically driven decisions.

Rory Sutherland, Vice Chairman of Ogilvy & Mather Group is a prolific thinker in many marketing facets and he has an interesting take on the future of agencies. To him, excessive bifurcation between media and creative and an obsession around data and quantifiable performance has led to the demise of the advertising industry.

"It's a nomothetic problem in our business. A large part of the value in advertising will never be predictable in advance or quantifiable in hindsight. A large part of marketing is probabilistic; you communicate to a million people because you don't know who's going to buy your product," says Sutherland. Obsessing over data and past performance is rarely indicative of future performance or future customer behaviour.

We've reached a point where agencies are operating with razor-thin margins, decisions to hire agencies are increasingly being made by procurement departments rather than marketing departments and there's a race to the bottom to provide cheap services.

"Agency account teams are chasing labour and managers are simply interested in bossing people around. This has created a culture where the ad industry is incentivized into insignificance. The kind of work being produced is low value, low margin and highly time-consuming. It's really within a narrow definition of value creation," says Sutherland.

"Most advertising problems are like Sudoku: you can't see them in separate blocks, you must see them together. The separation between media and creative was not good. Yes, it made us more money, but it disrupted the value. And the client was not included in the equation at all."

Sutherland believes it all began to topple with the obsession of digital and targeting. Media agencies relished the opportunity to finally seize backsome control over creative agencies and they did this by perpetuating the notion that data and targeting generated greater sales for advertisers. Of course, this is simply not true. With the rising prominence of *How Brands Grow* by Byron Sharpe, one of the leading pieces of literature in advertising today, we began to understand that highly targeted campaigns were in fact inversely correlated with brand growth. Sarcastically called "The Dark Lord of Penetration" by Mark Ritson, Sharpe's literature is focused on the need for mass, categorical penetration. It is one of the foundational tenets of CPG advertising – an industry that by its very definition needs to reach mass numbers of individuals to be effective. There is no single persona of a toothpaste buyer or a detergent buyer, hence why Colgate's advertising needs to appeal to wide swaths of the population. Mass advertising allows a brand to be top of mind when a prospective consumer is ready to convert.

How Brands Grow and other work around the importance of broad reach caused advertisers to begin questioning the effectiveness of their media mix. P&G, the world's largest advertiser, pulled ad dollars from Facebook in 2016 and reported a limited impact to sales as a result. Marc Pritchard, P&G's Chief Brand Officer and ruthless critic of Facebook initially commented that their practice of targeted advertising showed limited effectiveness, though he later admitted that the company took their strategy of targeting the right customers a bit too far.

"We targeted too much, and we went too narrow," he said in an interview, "and now we're looking at: What is the best way to get the most reach but also the right precision?"

There is still so much left to be understood about the way marketing works. But if you're in marketing today – and particularly if you work at an agency, you have an incredibly important job to do. Brands say that the single most important attribute that they seek in an agency partner is their ability to understand their industry. Industry insight and diagnosis into how a brand can effectively position itself and fit in are the foundational cornerstones of a decent strategy. There's a reason why strong strategy is rooted in a proper and fundamental understanding of the marketplace.

The question then becomes: if brands admit that foundational knowledge and industry nuances are important agency attributes, then how much are they willing to pay for it? At what point are we collectively, as marketers, going to shift away from the commoditization of the industry? How can we ensure we adequately pay for the nuances of experience, expertise and problem-solving abilities that we're asking from agencies?

On the flip side, performance models are becoming increasingly common. The notion being if it were a true partnership, the brand and the agency would be equally invested in helping the brand grow, with the agency's financial model tied to the performance of the brand. This makes sense in a vacuum. But marketing realities affect the outcome. Agencies are typically given limited sovereignty into aspects like website design, pricing or product – elements that arguably have more impact over performance than media and optimization.

While doing a recent stint in consultancy, a dog boarding and grooming franchise approached me with their plans to aggressively take over the U.S. As dog lovers, they had built their whole business model around providing dog owners with on-demand care and support for their pups. A decent business with decent potential. The problem? Their brand was completely unknown. Even for customers that may have heard of them, their website conveyed no important information on how to book services or even where to find the nearest location. I proposed they conduct research to understand their prospective audiences and create a decent brand positioning that would resonate with customers.

"We know having a brand that customers like is important. But we also need to show immediate ROI. So, scrap the brand stuff, and go heavy on the performance marketing," said their Director of Marketing.

This has become commonplace. The need to show aggressive quarter-over-quarter growth has led marketers to favour short-term tactics and results. Decades-worth of work on marketing effectiveness by renowned researchers like Binet & Field get pushed out the door in a split second, and marketers revert to the safe and easy conversion-based media plan. The problem, however, is that favouring short-term tactics inevitably plummets market share within a few short years.

For an effective relationship with an agency, brands need to relinquish a certain level of control to get the job done effectively. And agencies, in turn, need to prioritize formal training and constant re-skilling. Media planning and buying is one aspect of the job, but so is understanding how the industry and ecosystem functions as a whole – and why it matters when agencies choose to continue investing with partners like Facebook. For a while, we've encouraged "learning on the job" rather than any sort of formal training. But we know formal marketing training makes you a better marketer. Period. We need to spend the time to learn the discipline and craft of marketing.

My parents were steadfast in drilling in the importance of education. Everything we did was to set me up for a strong postgraduate education aimed at making me a more attainable prospect. My university experience was great, perhaps because I was naturally curious and relished the opportunity to learn. Even I admit, however, that university didn't instil the requisite skills needed to survive in the real working world. Understanding media strategy through continued exposure to academics and thought leaders in the field was half the battle – the other was learning the soft skills needed to effectively navigate through the corporate world.

Agency people have an important job to do today. As platforms proliferate and consolidate, where we choose to spend our clients' dollars matters. And it matters now more than ever. After leaving the agency world to explore client-side, I once again found myself back at an agency during the pandemic. I couldn't shake this feeling that I still had work to do agency-side.

I joined an organization called Arcane – a small marketing shop in London, Ontario – built around the premise that they weren't part of a massive holding company. They were born with the goal to help small and medium-sized businesses accelerate their marketing. When I joined, they were still relatively focused on performance marketing and tactics, delivering with extreme precision that ROI-focused narrative that clients loved to hear. What was unique about them, however, was that they had–hidden gem – an entire creative department, totally undervalued. Creative and brand came second to the performance marketing media plan, which was of course, the wrong way around. The other thing that was great about them was their commitment to taking on clients who shared their same ethical and moral values. At times, we would end up firing clients that were a clear mismatch for the company.

But one thing that remained difficult to reconcile was that despite hand-picking our clients and proudly talking about our ethical backbone, we continued to invest with Facebook. We made small progress through establishing partnerships with more transparent companies like The Trade Desk, but the largest proportion of our client's budgets continued to go to Facebook. In October 2021, another bomb fell on Facebook with the very public accusations made by whistle-blower Frances Haugen. She filed complaints with federal law enforcement, stating that during her time with Facebook she saw, "conflicts of interest between what was good for the public and what was good for Facebook." Very specifically, the complaints said Facebook's own research showed that it amplified hate, misinformation and political unrest – but the company hid what it knew. One complaint alleged that Instagram intentionally buried research that illustrated its harmful effects on teenage girls. This was the largest whistleblowing scandal in Facebook's history.

When this story broke, LinkedIn was flushed with advertising professionals shaking their heads at Facebook, damning their unethical practices. We collectively agreed that Facebook's practices were abhorrent and deplorable. But what would change from here? Would we, as agency people, finally decide to stop funnelling billions into a platform so blatantly harmful and damaging? Would clients combine their clout to boycott this increasingly menacing firm? Or would we continue onwards, effecting little change, continuing to complicitly fund this monster?

At Arcane, a large portion of our clients used Facebook and Instagram to drive e-commerce sales. Cutting them from their media plans was simply a big gamble that small businesses were not willing to take. Most of them still had no clear understanding between their ad dollars and supporting a platform that was accused of destabilizing countries or encouraging unhealthy teen choices. As education around this continues, my hope is that brands will begin to sever their ties with Facebook and re-invest their dollars into other, more responsible arenas.

So, what does the future hold for agencies? Without a crystal ball, it's tough to say with certainty, but what we do know, is that there will be greater importance placed on strategic expertise and industry knowledge moving forward. Agencies play a critical role in helping organizations shape the story of their brands, their customers, and their markets. It is also an opportunity for smaller independent agencies to differentiate themselves from bigger holding companies. They can critique and view things in a way that is not hindered by layers of organization and process. And we all have an immense obligation to spend our client's dollars ethically and responsibly.

In the current market, an agency needs to be diversified and they need to be relevant. A client's brief will always ask for the same thing: help my brand to grow. But the levers and strategies that you employ to do so will vary. Agency life is intertwined with change. Business and marketing are both changing dramatically because customers and expectations are changing. To continue to evolve, agencies must change – and there's nothing wrong with that. Many young, bright-eyed people land in advertising and quickly figure out they're drastically overworked, often questioning what value they receive from continuing to work there. Take it from someone who credits a significant amount of her knowledge and expertise to agency experience. Appreciate agency life for what it has to offer: a vast amount of learning opportunities across different clients and different types of businesses. It's for the endlessly curious, and it allows you to continuously feed a desire to learn.

Our industry is changing – we're once again at a crossroads. Agency people need to have a point of view on where we go from here. Because

Facebook is a monster in the making. And where we choose to invest advertising dollars matters. It matters now more than ever.

Chapter 5: Too Many Problems
Amina Qureshi

"[Facebook has] weaponized social media. They have weaponized the First Amendment. They have weaponized civic discourse. And most of all, they have weaponized politics."
- Kara Swisher

Today, information is accessible through the smartphones in our pockets – devices that contain more computing power than the Apollo 11 guidance computers that navigated the first man to the moon. The accessibility and pervasiveness of information democratize access to knowledge, which previously distinguished classes and castes, and was used to perpetuate socioeconomic status. After all, if your parents went to Ivy League schools, you are 45% more likely to attend one too. Because their likelihood to attend a selective school is higher, and they are, in turn, more likely to stress the importance of attending one to their own kids – the chasm between those with and without access to resources widens.

The advent of the iPhone in 2007 revolutionized the proliferation of access to information. And like anything else truly transformational, while it simultaneously solved existing problems, it introduced new ones. Over time, iPhones slowly became an extension of ourselves. That 4.8 oz device began encroaching on our limited supply of attention by always being available, and more often than not, physically attached to our bodies. In June 2014, when discussing a case on cell phone privacy, Chief Justice John Roberts wrote that modern smartphones have become so ingrained in daily life that "the proverbial visitor from Mars might conclude they were an important feature of human anatomy."

A new survey conducted by YouGov Omnibus confirms that this is not far from the truth. Just over 50% of millennials report that they now carry their phone in their hand throughout the day. On average, we tap, swipe and click our phones 2,617 times per day. It's undeniable that addiction to smartphones is a very real, very daunting thing. When smartphones became more than gadgets, they began to pose an addictive, attention-hijacking threat. Why? Quite simply, humans crave micro-feedback. Every time a notification pops up or a 'ding' from an iMessage comes through – we receive a hit of dopamine. The very same neurotransmitter that researchers have found plays an integral role in the formation of addiction to almost every illicit substance from cocaine and heroin to excessive alcohol use. Biologically, dopamine has a role to play in that it rewards us for working hard and accomplishing tasks. And it feels good to get rewarded. Our bodies begin to crave it. This same neurological process is replicated with technology each time our screen lights up with a notification. That notification serves as a proxy for social validation. The problem is that we need more of it to feel the same effect, therefore contributing to the addictive nature of digital rewards.

This is micro-feedback in action. Humans long to be noticed, to be credited, to experience recognition. As our societies become more insular and cocooned by gadgets and devices, as we sever our physical human ties to one another – we increasingly turn to smartphones to receive recognition and feedback, because we're getting less of it in person.

Chamath Palihapitiya, former VP of Platform & Monetization and later VP of Growth at Facebook was an early senior executive, and was responsible for engineering the explosive growth of the platform by acquiring new users and keeping the existing ones engaged. In 2017, he publicly spoke up about his "tremendous guilt" over growing the social network by any means necessary, which he believes has eroded "the core foundations of how people behave by and between each other."

Adding fire to the fuel, he reiterated that we are at a point now where "We have created tools that are ripping apart the social fabric of how society works. That is truly where we are. The short-term, dopamine-driven feedback loops that we have created are destroying how society works: no civil discourse, no cooperation, misinformation, mistruth. And it's not an American problem. This is not about Russian ads. This is a global problem."

Facebook issued an official response to both Palihapitiya's 2017 remarks as well as to The Social Dilemma. Both responses entail similar commentary counteracting accusations around social media addiction, user attention as a product, algorithms as insidiously robotic world domination machines, unsolicited data monetization and the proliferation of polarization and misinformation. In short, Facebook agreed that we should be having meaningful conversations around the impact of social media, but that sensationalized whistleblowing claims by former executives and Netflix documentaries bury the substance in hype.

They maintained that the platform prioritizes meaningful social interactions, and in a deliberate attempt to temper addiction, they've deprioritized viral videos, resulting in a decrease of 50M hours a day worth of time spent on Facebook. In a similar vein, YouTube publicly announced its attempt at minimizing the amplification of extreme content. But recommendation engines are one of the most powerful machine-learning systems today because of their ability to systematically shape the information we consume, process and believe.

They hijack our attention because they know what we are most apt to respond to. Just like any consumer-facing app, algorithms in recommendation engines provide relevant content to users based on their interests and preferences. Relevancy has become a digital currency and the more fine-tuned and finessed a piece of content is to the individual's tastes, the more an advertiser pays for it.

Has Facebook taken actionable steps to address the systemic problems rooted in addictive behaviors? Not in any meaningful way. Will they continue to rely on algorithmic functions to safeguard their user bases and rely on lucrative advertising models to continue growing? Our assumption is yes, perhaps accompanied by an ill-fated attempt at diversifying out of advertising. Will we reach a tipping point where our intellectual capabilities are put under existential threat by the very complex technologies and systems we created? Perhaps. But to mediate a solution requires a deeper understanding of how and why the concept of human attention is so important to Facebook.

Attention as digital currency

Attention as an empirical discipline has interested philosophers, psychologists, scientists and religious thinkers for centuries. The word "attention" is perceived differently by different people. At its very broadest, the study of attention is the study of conscious experience and the very sense of existence. Human attention, valuable and limited in supply, is a resource.

It has become commonplace, especially in the media and technology industries, to speak of an "attention economy" and of competition in "attention markets." There is even an attentional currency, the "basic attention token" (BAT) which purports to serve as a medium of exchange for user attention. Platforms like Facebook and Google, which have emerged as two of the most important platforms in the global economy, depend near exclusively on attention markets as a business model.

The Social Dilemma takes a hard and fast stance on how platforms use attentional currency: "If you are not paying for the product, you are the product." This suggests that while platforms are seemingly 'free' in that we don't pay for a subscription or any one-time fee to join, our experience within them and the data that we pass back to their algorithms comes at a substantive cost.

Facebook's official response posits that they have never sold data to any advertiser and that customer data privacy is at the heart of their legal, compliance and operational processes. But consumers may feel differently. Since the Cambridge Analytica scandal, consumer trust in Facebook dropped by 66%, with the majority of users saying they want explicit details on how and when their data is being shared.

Despite the well-recognized commercial importance of attention markets, the law has struggled when it's encountered this space. Antitrust agencies, tasked with assessing the effects of mergers and controlling anti-competitive behaviour, lack a way to understand the market dynamics when firms offer "free products" that are competing for attention. Meanwhile, those tasked with consumer protection have no paradigm for dealing with attentional intrusions stemming from non-consensual or intrusive advertising.

Facebook is certainly not the only digital player under massive scrutiny. As recent as October, 2020 – the U.S. Justice Department filed an antitrust lawsuit against Google. Though Europe has taken firmer action against Google by criticizing their anti-competitive actions, the U.S. has been slower to do so – until now.

Concentrating Power in the Hands of a Few

As we emerge from COVID-19, we understand just how many organizations suffered intolerable blows to their business. Many small and medium businesses filed for bankruptcy and shuttered for good. 225 million individuals lost their jobs. There were a few companies, however, that escaped unscathed. Not only did they emerge from the pandemic, but they also experienced unbridled growth during a time of significant economic downturn.

Technology giants such as Alphabet, Amazon and Apple are more dominant than pre-pandemic, thanks to greater reliance on their services during the pandemic. Quite simply, they've created products that demand utility. We can't imagine our lives without them.

The 2012 merger between Facebook and Instagram is a flagrant example of ambiguity when it comes to attention, competition and monopolistic practices. Here is the challenge: both firms offer social networks for sharing content, but neither company seems to charge end-consumers for their products. There has been no precedent established and therefore, the traditional tools for assessing potential anticompetitive effects don't work. If consumers don't "buy" Facebook or Instagram, then how can traditional economic tools tell us whether Facebook or Instagram are competing?

The Facebook-Instagram merger was approved based on two main premises. Firstly, Facebook did not have an important photo app   and therefore was not a serious competitor to Instagram in consumer markets. Secondly, Instagram was not yet earning advertising revenue and therefore was not a competitor to Facebook for advertisers.

And then there's the story around Facebook's merger with WhatsApp. WhatsApp's growth gobbled up user messaging and connection time that once could have belonged to Facebook. Now, those users and their time do belong to Facebook. Through merging, WhatsApp allows Facebook to both own the 'the next Facebook' and prevent 'the next Facebook from eating Facebook's lunch.'

For us to reign in large issues like data and privacy or teen bulimia and addiction, we need policy and lawmakers to take a stance. We need to identify these issues, assess their risk to individuals and society, and come to a solution-based consensus that mitigates negative impact, holding Facebook accountable. Coincidentally, while we were writing this book, the CEOs of the three biggest global tech companies were summoned by the Senate to testify on October 28, 2020.

Americans began demanding some answers.

Called to Justice

After the blunder of Cambridge Analytica, Facebook was allowed to walk away scot-free. This signified to the public that there was no accountability left. Facebook had legally weaselled their way out once again. But this time around, lawmakers and politicians openly and very bluntly acknowledged the danger that Facebook now posed to democratic societies globally if left unchecked.

Specifically, lawmakers in the U.S. revisited the legal shield that has long protected the tech industry. The legal shield in question, Section 230, was passed in the mid-90s – the early days of the Internet – and was intended to help tech companies grow by legally protecting them from content posted to their sites, such that they are not held to the same content standards as more traditional journalistic outlets. By definition, Section 230 is a section of Title 47 of the United States Code enacted as part of the United States Communications Decency Act, that generally provides immunity for website platforms with respect to third-party content.

The overarching conclusion from the Senate hearing was that while this law arguably made sense during the early days, it is now unilaterally absolving platforms from taking responsibility for conspicuous, hurtful, damaging and dangerous content – the spread of which is increasingly uncontrollable by advanced algorithms at play.

Mark Zuckerberg, Sundar Pichai and Jack Dorsey of Facebook, Alphabet (Google's parent company) and Twitter respectively, were questioned in depth about polarization, lack of fact-checking and selective censorship in the midst of the 2016 and 2020 election cycles.

"When the subject is net neutrality, these platforms warn against the grave threat of throttling the flow of information on the internet; meanwhile, these same companies are actively blocking and throttling the distribution of content on their own platforms and are using protections under Section 230 to do it. Reasonable observers are left to wonder whether big tech firms are obstructing the flow of information to benefit one political ideology or agenda. Our concern is that these platforms have become powerful arbiters of what is true and what content users can access. "The American public gets little insight into the decision-making process when content is moderated and users have little recourse when they are censored or restricted," said Chairman Roger Wicker in his opening remarks.

The Senate hearing was intended to increase the accountability of companies that engage in content moderation and to right-size their liability shield. But opening remarks from Senator Maria Cantwell insinuated that there were broader issues at hand than whether these platforms promote transparency, accountability and fairness in their content moderation process. How we harness the information age to work for us and not against us is something that we face every single day.

She argues there are also unaddressed issues of privacy as well as issues of whether there is truly a competitive news market to ensure diversity of voices and opinions. True competition helps perfect information both for global economies and for the health of democratic nations around the world. Clearly, it's not an issue that should be taken lightly. To her, tech companies are throttling publishing and news. The vertical nature of news and information creates a chokepoint whereby these outlets have seen more than a 70% reduction in revenues.

"Too much control in the advertising market limits the ability of media outlets to grow in the digital age. Just like other forms of media have made the transition, we want to have a dynamic and healthy news media," Cantwell says.

If we recall what happened in 2016, reports from the FBI, U.S. intelligence agencies and a bipartisan committee concluded that Russian operatives masqueraded as Americans. They employed targeted advertising, self-generated content, intentionally falsified news articles, and used social media platform tools to try and deceive tens of millions of people in the United States. They tampered with the election process and therefore destabilized the very democratic fabric of American society.

Director of National Intelligence and then former Senator Dan Coates said in 2016, "The warning lights are blinking red that the digital infrastructure that serves our country is under attack."

Cantwell's hope is that large-scale social platforms will provide some insight into what they've been doing to clamp down on election interference – specifically what processes have been implemented to curtail hate speech and misinformation.

"I will not tolerate people to continue to whack at our election process, our vote by mail system or the ability of tech platforms, security companies and collective communities to speak up against hate speech and misinformation. We have to show that the United States of America stands behind our principles and that our principles also transfer to the communication of information online… I know that people believe that these issues are out of sight and out of mind. I guarantee you that they are not. There are actors that have been at this for a long time by continuously sewing disinformation into society. I want to show them that we in the United States have fair elections, we do have a fair process and we will be the beacon of democracy," urges Cantwell.

"So I hope that as we speak about more than [Section] 230 today and the progress that [platforms have] made on the ways in which misinformation has been reduced today. What can we do on transparency?

On reporting? On analysis? On algorithms? And the kind of oversight that we all want, to ensure that we have a diversity of voices both online and offline," she continued.

Although the proposed regulations were still fuzzy and unclear, it finally seemed as though the government was intervening to curb Big Tech's unparalleled growth. It became apparent that the problems social platforms posed were no longer constrained to a handful of arbitrary individuals, but were symptomatic of larger collective dangers to democracy and society. These were very real problems with very real implications. And we were finally done brushing them under the rug.

Data: The New Gold Rush

In my early 30s, I found myself like a fish out of water. I had just returned back to work after taking a year off for maternity leave, and my head spun from how the industry changed so vastly in just the blink of an eye. "Data-driven marketing" was a buzzword all industry practitioners were quickly adopting to persuade brands that the right data points were being leveraged and activated in the right environments to drive business results. Our experience with data management platforms back then was cursory at best, and data was still quite siloed in individual walled garden environments. But the pace of advertising was picking up speed and I felt displaced when returning to work.

I was working with Canada's largest telecommunications brand at the time. It was a demanding job, with long hours. I was still breastfeeding my son and regularly had to sneak into conference rooms to pump before moving onto the next meeting or deliverable. It was stressful and exhausting and I was challenged to keep up. Eventually, I threw in the towel and quit. It was liberating and I felt that I could finally breathe again. I didn't have an immediate opportunity lined up, but I didn't care.

An industry friend of mine eventually introduced me to a burgeoning opportunity at Loblaw Companies Limited – Canada's largest retailer. They had amassed a large 1st party data set through their loyalty program, *PC Optimum,* and were looking to commercialize the program. The idea behind it was to leverage the data points from the 19M Canadians enrolled in the loyalty program for better targeting and better measurement for marketing activities. I was tasked with setting up the business unit to support the initiative called Loblaw Media. If data was the new frontier in advertising, I had struck gold.

The obsessive pursuit with the collection of personalized data has obviously come under massive scrutiny in the last few years. Not simply because of large-scale data breaches like Cambridge Analytica, but the quieter, more nefarious implications of seeding excessive personalized data. Platforms would contend that users provide informed consent when they sign up for their accounts. Academics like Dr. Carissa Véliz from the Institute for Ethics in AI at the University of Oxford argues that there is no such thing as informed consent when it comes to technology. This is because future uses of data are largely unforeseen, even by the very data scientists employed by technology companies themselves. If we can't imagine how our data will one day be used, how are we able to give informed consent? Quite simply: we can't.

In Azeem Azhar's podcast titled Should We End the Data Economy?, he invites Dr. Véliz to articulate what is wrong with the data economy and whether we should outwardly ban trading-in personal data. Online data is far more of a problem than irritating personalized ads for embarrassing products and dodgy loans. The sheer scale of personal data circulating on the internet cannot be underestimated, and it is undermining equality and democracy.

In the podcast and in Dr. Véliz's new book, Privacy is Power, she argues that we are now subjects of a powerful data world, which goes right to the heart of economies and democratic government, and over which we have too little control. She calls for an end to the data economy. Personal data, she argues, is not the kind of thing that should be allowed to be bought and sold.

Every time you engage with tech, or tech engages with you, the data economy intrudes into your life, according to Dr Véliz, who warns about the vast amount of data now collected on everyone. It is not just your likes and dislikes and purchases. It's who your friends and family are, what time you get up in the morning, where you spent last night, how much money you have in the bank, whether you are unwell, how much you drink, how much you weigh, what you search for online. A virtual avatar of you can be created from every keystroke you make on your computer or your mobile phone, accumulating information about you. That data is then used to try to influence your behaviour – from what you buy to how you vote.

And it all may seem totally innocuous. Until that data reaches the wrong hands. To illustrate the disastrous impacts of hoarding significant amounts of personal data, Dr. Véliz explains how the Nazis were able to utilize generational data in different countries to find Jews and send them to concentration camps.

"To collect as much personal data as possible and keep it for as long as possible is reckless. It's even a danger from the point of view of national security. It is a ticking bomb," Dr. Véliz says.

"Before the Second World War, the Netherlands kept careful records of its population's religious affiliation. It meant that the Nazis, by looking through registries, were able to locate and murder approximately 73% of the Jewish population. But, in France, by contrast, where they did not keep such records for privacy reasons, it was not as easy to know who was Jewish – although the Nazis were still able to find and assassinate approximately 25% of the Jewish population in France," she continues.

This grave but important example suggests that countries, organizations and systems should not be allowed to keep unnecessary troves of personalized data. Inevitably, it will end up in the wrong hands or used in situations beyond its intended purpose. The podcast does a nice job of laying out the issues at hand, while simultaneously suggesting valid solutions. As part of her solutions framework, Dr. Véliz proposes to outright ban data trades. When evaluating the pros alongside the cons, it's clear that the risks of data trades far outweigh any perceived or real benefits.

And there is an even greater threat outside of the advertising industry. In a Yuval Noah Harari-esque construct, the problem with data and fine- tuned messaging isn't limited to any one industry. For him, the problem is a philosophical and existential threat to humanity. It's created a space where there is no such thing as free will. Any individual thoughts, beliefs and desires are the results of being targeted by algorithms far more advanced than human cognition. Harari often cites an anecdotal example of discovering his homosexuality quite late in life. He believes that algorithms could have predicted this far before his own consciousness did, based on his online behaviour and physiological signals. If this is truly the case, and we are at the mercy of machines, then free will is a fallacy.

If this sounds like something out of a science fiction novel, it's not. With the growth of machine learning, computational algorithms are processing information at intense speeds. The more logical part of our brain kicks in to counteract the notion that we have no control over our lives. That we are the by-product of a handful of algorithms. The human brain is an incredibly impressive organ. It can process more information than even the fastest computer, and it's 100,000 times more energy efficient.

It's an extraordinarily complex organ that's capable of accomplishing platitudes. Why then, is it so easily malleable and controllable? If Yuval Noah Harari is right, if YouTube really could have predicted that he would one day acknowledge his homosexuality, how far down the rabbit hole have we gone? Is there any hope of re-emerging and gaining back control over our own cognition? And how much blame should be given to advertising and marketing when there are arguably so many factors contributing to the hijacking of human thought and emotion?

The answer lies in how well-shrouded in mystery our own mind is. Our pursuit to understand ourselves has likely been around since the dawn of homosapiens. Perhaps back then, the nagging idea of "who am I?" was not as prevalent, because humans were wrapped up in thwarting dangers and ensuring their livelihood and safety. But it was still there. Every generation before us yearned to know more, therefore expanding their cognition and intelligence. Yet even today, the human brain is a modern-day marvel and remains almost as much a mystery as it always was. For Harari, the only way out is to attain a level of deep, meditative understanding of one's own mind. To focus on our internal world by quieting our chatterbox of a brain and unravelling hidden layers of consciousness. These always seemed like words on a page, until I tried it myself. Over the years, through disciplined practice, meditation has become one of the only ways of re-centring and rebalancing myself, particularly in a world that seems to be getting more chaotic as it evolves.

It wasn't always like that. I spent my 20s working my way up within roles of increasing importance, yet I was anxious and constantly tired. If I was honest with myself back then, I was unhappy. When I wasn't pitching digital advertising to my Fortune 100 clients, I would be scrolling Instagram, comparing my life to others', craving those little red notifications that signalled my social worth. I continued to interact with content online by parsing back digital signals about my likes, dislikes, fears and anxieties. Over time, my news feed became more and more homogenous. Continuously serving up content that filled the bottomless echo-chamber of my pre-existing notions and beliefs. It was rare to see something I vehemently disagreed with.

A few years later, it dawned on me that if these algorithms were a mystery to me – to somebody who had spent a decade and a half in the industry – then it must be a total black box to the general public. It was only once I suspended my social media accounts, restricted YouTube to morning runs only, and made a concerted effort to minimize time on my iPhone overall that I realized just how addicted I was. I found that I had more time to think and to write – two activities that bring me immense joy. Maybe Harari was onto something after all. By simply quieting the mind and focusing, I was able to bring myself to a state of calm.

Relinquishing social media allowed me the time to think critically about the advertising industry and the impact that Facebook, in particular, was having on our world. There's an inherent tension in exploring these topics and unearthing the wrongs of Facebook. My entire professional life is intertwined with them. But as the uneasiness grew, and the noise became deafening, I knew I had to act.

Big Tech's Empathy Problem

We've reached a crossroads. Has technology progressed past humanity's most noble pursuits? Is it time to put on the brakes and re-evaluate how to regulate the technology industry to make it right again? We seem to have reached a point where the industry poses an empathy deficit. Maëlle Gavet, a leading technology executive and former CEO of Ozon, known colloquially as "The Amazon of Russia" is one of many voices to rallying for a clear call to action from industry leaders, board members, employees, and consumers to drive the change necessary to create better, more sustainable businesses.

Gavet examines the world of tech start-ups in the United States and Europe – from Amazon, Google and Facebook to Twitter, Airbnb, and Uber. In her opinion, the problematic issues that have risen out of Big Tech are due largely to four main reasons: Silicon Valley's cultural insularity, the hyper-growth business model, the sector's stunning lack of diversity, and a dangerous self-sustaining ecosystem. However, for her, it's not sufficient to simply take account of how an entire industry came off the rails. She also believes that we need a passionate call to action on how to get it back on track.

What are the steps Western governments are likely to take should tech leaders fail to do so? She believes these steps include reformed tax codes, reclassification of platforms as information companies, new labour laws, algorithmic transparency, and oversight.

The News Feed is the clearest example of a hyper-personalized environment engineered through sophisticated algorithms. Each time we interact with a certain type of content, the platform's algorithm will continue serving that same type of content in a self-perpetuating manner. Some may challenge why hyper-personalized algorithms are a bad thing. Isn't increased relevancy a good thing? An expectation that things will go badly is not, on the surface, any more or less rational than the expectation that things will go well. The problem is both universal and infinitely individualized.

The fundamental argument against algorithms lies in the cyclical dissemination of misinformation. When spread at such a rapid pace, with little to no oversight, misinformation has resulted in untenable misactions – from Russians impacting the last U.S. presidential election to genocide in Myanmar. Even the nomenclature of a "news feed" used on some social networks is curious, given that a significant portion of its content is not "news" in any conventional sense. This emphasis owes more to the idealistic history of the web as an "information superhighway," but like the emphasis on sociality, it obscures the timeline for other more common, maybe even dysfunctional purposes.

The Next Frontier

What's clear is the damage Facebook has caused up until this point. What began as a beautiful promise to connect the world's disparate communities has evolved into a political, attention-hijacking weapon of mass distraction. Sean Parker, an early investor, and proponent of Facebook, accused the social media giant of intentionally exploiting a vulnerability in human psychology. It remains to be seen how intentional Zuckerberg's blueprint for the company was, but what's definite is that we're embarking on a new frontier, one in which we must remedy the mistakes of the past to create a more connected future.

Chapter 6: Creating a Monster
Amina Qureshi

"The best way to differentiate the good from the bad is to look at economic incentives. Companies that sell you a physical product or a subscription are far less likely to abuse your trust than a company with a free product that depends on monopolizing your attention. The platforms are led by really smart, well-intentioned people, but their success took them to places where their skills no longer fit the job. They have created problems they cannot solve."

- Roger McNamee

Some people call Mark Zuckerberg a modern-day marvel – a young, astute Harvard student who created the world's most prolific social media platform. Some call him greedy, naive and self-centred. I believe even the most negatively polarized view of him doesn't deliver on the endangerment he's created and continues to perpetuate. Why does a man, who is currently worth $116B, continue to put revenue and growth above the collective good of its 3 billion users?

Controlling 58% of voting shares, Zuckerberg is allowed to do and say as he pleases. The problem, however, is that these decisions have compounding ripple effects outside of the walls of 1 Hacker Way: they've caused political destabilization, encouraged teen eating disorders and undermined the institutions responsible for maintaining the democratic health of our society. These aren't unsubstantiated accusations by a handful of disgruntled employees. They are known, factual, intentional, choiceful decisions that are a direct by-product of Zuckerberg's decision to throttle the truth about his company's actions.

And he must be stopped.

When we sat down to chat with David Carroll – one of the best-known crusaders for data protection rights in the U.S and infamously involved in the Cambridge Analytica litigation – we straight off the bat asked him what can be done. His response surprised me. Rather than reiterating the perceived solution, whether it be government regulation or boycotting the platform, he instead asked: "Why wasn't it a bigger deal than it was? Why wasn't there global outrage from anyone who owned a Facebook account at the time? Or any brand who advertised on Facebook at the time?"

And his answer to his own question was equally interesting. It goes back to the old advertising adage that is so overused in our industry; the famous John Wanamaker quote: "Half the money I spend on advertising is wasted; the trouble is I don't know which half." The quote drives home the wastefulness of spray and pray traditional advertising. In contrast, digital advertising was designed as a gleaming beacon of hope to finally bring accountability and measurability to the practice.

According to Carroll, there wasn't a global outrage because most marketers still believe in the system. Facebook advertising is still the holy grail in measuring advertising effectiveness, and marketers downplay the impact of the grossly fraudulent organization that it's become. Carroll has a point. Marketers continue to invest in Facebook long after the Cambridge Analytica scandal broke, because they still believe that Facebook and the like offers one of the only ways to link their advertising efforts back to sales.

What Carroll went on to say still haunts me today. "Simply put, advertisers and marketers are completely trapped in trying to solve Wanamaker's rule, and the more they try, the more it causes unintentional consequences that prevent them from achieving this goal. So the radical proposition for advertising and marketing today is to admit that Wanamaker's rule is a law – you cannot defeat it. It is like a law of nature. It is like gravity. The more you try to eliminate the waste in advertising, the more it will haunt you. And you may not want to admit that it's happening, but it's happening. Whether it's fraud, or misinformation, or fake news, or the declining trust that humans have in government and journalism. These are all the downstream effects of trying to fix Wanamaker's law."

The outrage (or lack thereof) that Carroll was referring to, of course, was the Cambridge Analytica scandal. Though the same lack of outrage could be said of the multitude of scandals that followed, most recently Haugen's confession at the time of publishing this book. There is a blanket fear in marketing that pulling dollars from Facebook will lead to a decline in sales. Marketers haven't yet stopped to question whether the measurability was flawed and fraudulent to begin with. We're so deeply entangled in the weeds of the Facebook propaganda machine that brand marketers and agencies alike aren't pausing to peel back the layers in the narrative. This is dangerous. It's a dangerous position to occupy, because as marketers, we're turning a blind eye to the second-degree effects of investing in a platform that continues to cause societal damage.

If you're like most people, Cambridge Analytica probably rings a bell. You associate it with some vague indiscretion on Facebook's part that had to do with some data misuse. But let me tell you what actually happened. In the 2010s, personal data belonging to millions of Facebook users was collected without their consent by British consulting firm, Cambridge Analytica. 87 million users to be exact. This data was then used to target users for political campaigns on Facebook.

In fact, the data collected on users – including what type of content they interacted with – could tell with precise certainty which political party a user belonged to. The New York Times posted an article in 2016 titled Liberal, Moderate or Conservative? See How Facebook Labels You. It provided step-by-step instructions on how to access a user's profile to determine which party Facebook categorized them within:

"You may think you are discreet about your political views. But Facebook, the world's largest social media network, has come up with its own determination of your political leanings, based on your activity on the site."

And now, it is easy to find out how Facebook has categorized you – as very liberal or very conservative, or somewhere in between.

Try this: Go to facebook.com/ads/preferences on your browser. (You may have to log in to Facebook first.) That will bring you to a page with your ad preferences. Under the "Interests" header, click the "Lifestyle and Culture" tab.

Then look for a box titled "US Politics." In parentheses, it will describe how Facebook has categorized you – liberal, moderate or conservative."

The data was collected through an app called "This Is Your Digital Life"; developed by data scientist Aleksandr Kogan and his company Global Science Research in 2013. The app consisted of a series of questions to build psychological profiles on users, and collected the personal data of the users' Facebook friends via Facebook's Open Graph platform. The app harvested the data of about 87 million Facebook profiles. Cambridge Analytica then used the data to provide analytical assistance to the 2016 presidential campaigns of Ted Cruz and Donald Trump. Cambridge Analytica was also widely accused of interfering with the Brexit referendum, although the official investigation recognized that the company was not involved "beyond some initial enquiries" and that "no significant breaches" took place.

Information about the data misuse taking place was revealed by a Cambridge Analytica employee, Christopher Wylie, in 2018. He approached The Guardian and The New York Times, and over a series of interviews, disclosed just how bad the situation had become. In fact, Facebook's data misuse had political implications beyond the U.S. They were found to be linked to Russia.

In a companion piece, The Times reported that while working on their Facebook-derived profiles, people at Cambridge Analytica were in contact with executives from Lukoil, the Kremlin-linked oil giant. Lukoil was interested in the ways data was being used to target American voters, according to two former company insiders. Cambridge Analytica and Lukoil denied that the talks were political in nature and said the oil giant never became a client.

What's more, undercover footage of Cambridge Analytica's Chief Executive Officer, Alexander Nik, was released by a British television channel. It captured him saying the company had used methods of seduction and bribery to entrap politicians and sway political outcomes. Of course back in Washington, this started to stir the pot. They were already suspicious of, and actively investigating Facebook's role in manipulating the Trump campaign. Now more interference with Russians? Congress finally demanded some answers and summoned Zuckerberg to testify.

It became clear, even back then, that Facebook intended on building an internal public relations and communications team, the likes of which were unheard of in organizations prior. A team put together to continuously and meticulously dig Facebook outof holes time after time. After a long and deafening silence from Zuckerberg on the issue, he finally responded five days later.

It took almost an entire week for the founder and CEO of Facebook – the man with total control over the world's largest communications platform – to emerge from his Menlo Park cloisters and address the public. When he finally did, he did so with gusto, taking a new set of talking points ("We have a responsibility to protect your data, and if we can't then we don't deserve to serve you") on a seemingly unending roadshow – from his own Facebook page, to the mainstream press, to Congress.

The culmination of all that verbosity came when Zuck unloaded a 3,000-word treatise on Facebook's "privacy-focused" future (a phrase that somehow demands both regular quotation marks and ironic scare quotes), a missive that was perhaps best described by the Guardian's Emily Bell as "the nightmarish college application essay of an accomplished sociopath".

And even after all this, in 2022, we find ourselves having forgotten what actually happened. Somehow, yet again, we've forgiven Facebook for its misdoings and moved on. Indiscretion after indiscretion, scandal after scandal, Facebook's stock price continues to look like this:

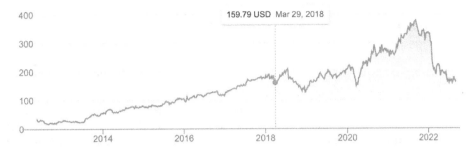

After facing a small, almost unnoticeable dip in March 2018 when the Cambridge Analytica scandal broke – it continued to climb aggressively and in fact, has doubled its March 2018 value as of October 2021. Not only did Facebook not stagnate or decline, but its user base also doubled – from 1.5B in 2018 to almost 3B today. Advertising dollars kept flowing in, amounting from $50B in 2018 to $82B in 2020. Even after the largest data scandal in history broke and we knew with undeniable certainty that Zuckerburg intentionally allowed it to happen, brands continued to invest an extra 30 odd billion dollars.

What about the users? Can't we collectively band to deactivate our accounts across Facebook, Instagram and WhatsApp? The global population is primed for paranoia and anxiety, but users can't boycott impactfully because they're not the customer – advertisers are the customer. When users do boycott, it's a symptom of the trust crisis, but it's not actually affecting Facebook's bottom line. Even when WhatsApp loses tens of millions of users, it's still the dominant messaging platform. Consumers would need to enact a coordinated, mass insurgency against Facebook to have any meaningful impact, and let's be real – that's highly unrealistic.

Surely then, the answer lies with technology companies like Apple? As the dominant operating system in many global countries, could suffocating Facebook in its supply chain put a dent in Facebook's continued growth? With Apple recently doubling down on privacy, allowing its users to opt out of IDFA (the unique identifier advertisers use to target customers), they've strategically positioned themselves to thwart Facebook in its tracks. Whether the move on Apple's part was suspiciously self-serving to redirect advertising dollars towards their own ad ecosystem remains to be seen. In the meantime, the short-term impact of Apple's IDFA move is reflected in Facebook's Q3 2021 results.

Between Q2 - Q3 2021, Facebook's revenue dipped 2%. And while 2% may seem negligible, revenue growth between Q2 2020 - Q3 2020 reflected an increase from \$18.7B to 21.5B, and historic prior years have seen similar massive seasonal increases between the two quarters. So did it have an impact? Most definitely. The more interesting part of their earnings report is the story around ARPU (Average Revenue Per User). While the overall ARPU showed \$10.12 to \$10 between Q2 and Q3 2021 respectively, once we examine the impact of specific markets, the story continues to evolve. The overall ARPU may show a slight decrease quarter-on-quarter, however, there is a considerable drop in ARPU for iOS heavy markets like U.S., Canada and Europe. Contrastingly, Facebook's ARPU for Android heavy markets like APAC, MENA & LATAM had considerable increases. With APAC, MENA & LATAM being the fastest-growing markets for Facebook with significant room for growth, Facebook revenues are projected to remain stable in the near future. Unless, of course, Google decides to pull a similar move with Android – which seems unlikely.

Okay, so Apple and other technology giants may have somewhat of an impact, but that impact seems nominal and limited. What about actual Facebook employees? Surely, they have insight into the questionable dealings inside the firm. Frances Haugen's exposé of tens of thousands of internal Facebook documents is markedly different from previous accusations or scandals surrounding the company. For one, Haugen seems to possess the perfect profile for a whistle-blower. She was a former product manager on Facebook's civic integrity team, has held numerous positions in other Big Tech firms and she expresses her concern over Facebook's gross missteps in a calm, collected demeanour. The documents she brought to the light suggest that Facebook executives were fully aware of, and intentionally suppressed the research and data around Instagram's correlation to teen depression and suicide.

"There were conflicts of interest between what was good for the public and what was good for Facebook. And Facebook, over and over again, chose to optimize for its own interests, like making more money," said Haugen in the 60 Minutes interview in October 2021.

Haugen's exposé goes down as one of the most meticulously led media rollouts in history. Haugen first met Jeff Horwitz, a tech-industry reporter for The Wall Street Journal, early in December 2020 on a hiking trail in Oakland, California. She appreciated his thoughtfulness as a reporter, and he appreciated her candour in her writings on Facebook's role in transmitting Hindu nationalism in India. In short, they trusted each other. She wasn't just another whistle-blower, and he wasn't just another sensationalistic journalist on the hunt for the next big tech story. She got the impression that he would support her as a person, rather than as a mere source who could supply him with the inside information that she had picked up during her nearly two years as a product manager at Facebook.

She began disclosing tens of thousands of internal documents, which were revealed in an 11-article series craftily dubbed by the Wall Street Journal as "The Facebook Files." Key revelations included how Facebook executives handled politicized lies, including Donald J. Trump's claims of election fraud. Often, the company chose to let misinformation spread widely, to keep more people logging on. The series also noted the lengths that Facebook went to in its desperation to hang on to its audience as young people drifted away from its platforms.

"During my time at Facebook I realized a devastating truth: almost nobody outside of Facebook knows what happens inside Facebook. They operate in the dark," Haugen said in a statement.

That one sentence encapsulates so much truth. Even those who work in the industry don't know or fail to acknowledge the goings-on within the walls of Facebook. Brands and media agencies who complicitly invest billions globally, continue to do so with little to no knowledge about the inner workings or operations that perpetuate prioritizing growth and profits over the wellbeing of our communities.

"They win by keeping their systems closed without oversight or transparency, by shrouding their operations in secrecy and PR spin. I came forward because I believe that every human being deserves the dignity of the truth – and the truth is that Facebook buys its astronomical profits by sacrificing our safety. But it does not have to be this way – these problems are solvable. We can have the social media we love that also brings out the best in humanity," said Haugen in a March 2022 interview with ABC.

Like many of the serious global issues that plague us today, Internet safety is challenging because it's not confined to any specific border or country. It exists in a world – a meta world – in which the laws and order of the physical world do not apply. The political and legal structures of the physical world are simply too antiquated. But Haugen's confession was an important first step in creating a deep plea for policymakers to wake up. The time is now to begin understanding the unintended impact of social media, not in the rear-view mirror when circumstances have evolved to the point of being too dire to curtail.

Of particular importance, Haugen's confession laid bare Instagram's (which is owned by Facebook) impact on children. In one of her leaked documents, an internal Facebook study found that 13.5% of U.K. teen girls, in one survey, said their suicidal thoughts became more frequent after starting on Instagram. Another leaked study found 17% of teen girls say their eating disorders got worse after using Instagram. About 32% of teen girls said that when they felt bad about their bodies, Instagram made them feel worse, Facebook's researchers found. This was first reported by the Journal.

Sen. Marsha Blackburn, R-Tenn., accused Facebook of intentionally targeting children under the age of 13 with an "addictive" product – despite the app requiring users be 13 years or older.

"It is clear that Facebook prioritizes profit over the well-being of children and all users," she said.

Subcommittee Chair Richard Blumenthal, D-Conn., echoed this concern. What's interesting to note is Blackburn and Blumenthal represent different ends of the political spectrum but are united in their belief that Facebook and other social media giants should be regulated.

"Facebook exploited teens using powerful algorithms that amplified their insecurities," Blumenthal said. "I hope we will discuss as to whether there is such a thing as a safe algorithm."

And as if its disastrous impact on teenage girls wasn't extensive enough, the files continued to reveal Facebook's involvement in the prevalence of anti-vaccine misinformation in comments on Facebook posts, and the use of Facebook for the trafficking of vulnerable domestic workers.

In the end, what impact did Haugen's confession have on Facebook's stock price? It certainly made a dent. The stock price dipped below the $1 trillion mark, which it previously breezed past for the first time earlier in 2021. As Haugen took the dais in Parliament in late October 2021, analysts disagreed on whether her testimony and leaked documents could damage the tech giant. But by February 15, 2022's earnings call, Zuckerberg, undoubtedly feeling the pressure of continued public scrutiny, announced his boldest move yet: to rebrand his firm as Meta. Since then, the company's stock remains about 31% below where it initially stood at the outset of the announcement to rebrand.

But as marketing professor, academic and heavy Meta critic, Scott Galloway often jokes, Facebook might be "mendacious as fuck... but they're not stupid. This isn't 'putting lipstick on a pig.'" This move was deliberate, exacting, and intentionally constructed to shift the public eye away from their increasingly tarnished reputation.

In the weeks to follow, Galloway and tech journalist Kara Swisher extensively discussed Meta's rebrand on their podcast Pivot. Below is an excerpt from their conversation, which elegantly captures the notion that Facebook's rebrand is indicative of a larger organizational shift for the firm:

Galloway: Look, I think Facebook is mendacious. I think they demonstrate a lot of sociopathy, a lack of regard for the commonwealth. But they're not dumb. And right now, they're in a canyon and there's tsunamis of shit pouring down for them everywhere. And I imagine more than one person has said, "We need what I would call a blood offering. We need a dramatic change here. And Mark, you need to disassociate." I mean, an attorney general just added him personally to a suit. So I think he's basically decided, I need to disassociate and distinguish and put a ring fence around my involvement. I need the overlap between Mark Zuckerberg and Facebook to be less of an overlap. And I'm going to create a new brand architecture. I'm going to put someone in charge of Facebook so I can pretend it's not my fault and I'm going to go on morning shows with Oculuses, which is a lot less toxic.

Swisher: But can he do that? Everyone knows he has full control over everything. Can he actually pull it off? In the case of Alphabet, you know, Larry Page just, I think, didn't want to talk to people. And there were no PR people at Alphabet – like, you couldn't reach them, so you could never understand where the real power was, and that was the point. But I think in that case, there wasn't a particular controversy they were trying to avoid.

You know, I think they were just doing the first thing, which was giving people – Susan was the CEO of YouTube and Sundar Pichai was CEO of Google, and I get that part of it. And they did this at AOL many years ago – there was always a CEO of one of the divisions, right? It was a way to sprinkle around benefits to people, I guess. But this one – I think he cannot be disengaged from Facebook. Can he?

Galloway: Well, another thing I agree with you on. No one should go for the head fake, but I think it's a smart strategy. He wants to reposition himself around something more benign. He wants to distance himself from Facebook, and he wants to reposition, if you will, or increase the positioning of the company and him personally around, quote-unquote, the Metaverse. It's much less toxic. It's much more hopeful. It's much more visionary. And then at a minimum, he'll probably get out of a couple summons or calls to come speak in front of the House Antitrust Subcommittee because they will argue – and the committee will go for it – that, "Well, you should speak to the CEO of Facebook. That's the right person to come to." I hope people don't fall for it.

This excerpt, once again, paints Zuckerberg as a dangerous, deliberate sociopath. Centrists or supporters of Zuckerberg largely argue that these issues were unintended and unfortunate consequences of a social technology that nobody, especially Zuckerberg, had the foresight to control. And while it's debatable whether he set out to create a monster, the fact remains that he created one, a very public, very harmful monster – and unleashed it by assuming zero responsibility for what happens in the aftermath.

Digging into my background in journalism, I find the moral and ethical side of the argument an interesting one: should social media firms be treated (and therefore scrutinized) by the same yardstick as publishers and news outlets? The Spotify and Joe Rogan issue that blew up in January 2022 is another tentpole example of the polarized belief around whose responsibility it is to police the accuracy and legitimacy of content on social platforms. Facebook let vaccine misinformation go awry on its platform – but is it their fault? Spotify refused to censor or remove Rogan despite verified accusations against Rogan spreading vaccine misinformation. For Spotify, Rogan's podcast is a cash cow: it reaches an estimated 11 million listeners per episode- easily the streaming service's most popular podcast. For Facebook, misinformation posts receive six times as many likes, shares, and interactions as legitimate news articles.

In short, fake news makes money. Click-worthy headlines, despite how inaccurate, draw attention. The financial incentives that make Facebook and Spotify profitable don't align with assuming ethical responsibility for inflammatory content. These firms have shown themselves to be resistant to self-regulation. It's much easier to turn a blind eye to the problem, point a finger towards antiquated legislation and hope that lawmakers continue operating under the guise of naivety. Again, it begs the very simple question: who is ultimately responsible for policing content on social platforms?

If you ask me, I argue it's the responsibility and remit of the government to curtail Big Tech through legislation and regulation. And interestingly, both political parties in the United States are keen on doing so. However, there is no neat or simple solution to mitigating Facebook's unprecedented corporate, social, and political power. There is increasing consensus that antitrust action – or breaking up Facebook – would most likely just fracture the problem into smaller pieces, making the issues harder to tackle.

"We don't need to break them up; we need to break them open," said Tom Wheeler, former chairman of the Federal Communications Commission during the Obama administration.

There are two recent proposals that have legitimacy in addressing and solving these issues:

- Creating a new federal agency dedicated to Big Tech oversight.
- Senators are considering how to create independent oversight of major platform companies, but Tom Wheeler isn't confident that existing government agencies are up to the task.

"I ran an independent regulatory agency," he said, and the regulatory process "is sclerotic and rigid." "Now," he added, "we're moving at exponential speed in a world that was built for linear transformation."

Wheeler is calling for "a new agency of digital experts that has the agility to deal with the ever-evolving digital market." His proposition certainly has merit: the agency would bring tech industry leaders into dialogue with federal representatives (ideally digital natives) to determine an agreed-upon set of behavioural standards, later codified and enforced by the agency through monitoring, monetary penalties and disgorgement. Unlike existing agencies, Wheeler argues, a new agency created from scratch would allow the implementation of modern management practices and policies capable of keeping pace with a fast-moving industry.

Stricter privacy legislation to limit Facebook's power

Siva Vaidhyanathan, director of the Center for Media and Citizenship at the University of Virginia, believes a new federal agency won't solve this monstrous problem. Vaidhyanathan takes a more international perspective on the issue, arguing that Facebook is not "going to change its behavior because of something that happens in the United States." More than 3.5 billion people around the world use Facebook's platforms, and in some countries like India, by itself home to over 300 million users, the company is synonymous with the internet. "When Mark Zuckerberg wakes up in the morning, I guarantee you he thinks about India before he thinks about the United States," Vaidhyanathan said.

The company also applies different policies and algorithms in different legal jurisdictions, and the United Kingdom and the European Union are each exploring additional platform regulation. So instead of focusing on regulations that would affect only the United States, Vaidhyanathan argues, lawmakers would be more effective in going after the company's primary source of profit: personal data.

"We could pass strong legislation in the United States and encourage other countries to follow the same route that would severely limit what companies, not just Facebook and Google, but all companies, do in terms of surveillance and the use of our data," he said. There would naturally be some exceptions, such as public health data. Siva said that forcing companies to delete the personal data of their users within a set window of time would limit ad targeting and algorithmic amplification, making both "less precise and less effective."

Of course, as someone who works and makes a living from the advertising industry – this latter proposal makes me nervous. It reflects the very real, very torn stance I am regularly faced with: am I an active enabler of an industry that is wrought and wrangled with questionable practices around data and privacy? Late in 2021, I started a new job at LinkedIn. I had always wanted to grow into Tech, but knew I could never stomach working for Facebook. LinkedIn's mission always resonated with me: to provide economic opportunity for every member of the global workforce. This isn't a platform making money off trolls and clickbait. Despite the vast troves of 1st party data, this isn't a company regularly accused of abusing it. In fact, they were one of the first companies to ban political advertising. It defines political ads as including "ads advocating for or against a particular candidate or ballot proposition or otherwise intended to influence an election outcome."

In a nutshell: they believe it's unethical to use targeted advertising to sway a certain political outcome. They're an emblematic example of an organization that balances profit, power and assumes responsibility for the public commonwealth. And it's no easy task. Particularly when Wall Street hungrily comes knocking on your door for aggressive quarter-over-quarter growth. In short, they're a company that's made me realize I can continue on in the advertising industry, an industry I've come to know, love and have a deep passion for. I can finally reconcile the uncomfortable truth that the industry was largely built on questionable practices, but there is still room for good players to succeed. Sure, I may be biased because that's where I work – but the public seems to agree. LinkedIn was named the most trusted social media platform for the fifth year in a row, according to eMarketer's Digital Trust Benchmark Report 2021.

Trust is arguably the most important characteristic of brand equity: can your customers rely on you? Have you proven that you operate with their best interests at heart? Customers today are savvy and younger generations are becoming savvier. Companies that operate selfishly and unilaterally are called out and actively boycotted against. And LinkedIn, amongst all the sensationalist headlines occupied by their competitors in blue, remain an enigma.

Despite its massive size – nearly 800 million global members – this platform isn't filled with the same type of misinformation, trolls, and engagement-baiting algorithms that define its peers. The tone on LinkedIn is, actually, kind of friendly. It's a place, as Scott Galloway recently put it, where people assume you're engaging in good faith, not bad. "I no longer respond to people on any platform except LinkedIn," Galloway said. "People are much more civil." And there's a reason for this. Actually, there are many.

The main reason is that your boss, your colleagues and the community that will largely influence how far you will succeed in your career – are actively present. People don't behave like shitheads because there's an identity tied to their words – and a scrutinizing community of real-life professionals waiting. Trolling suddenly isn't an option when you have to own up to it with your bonafied peers. But LinkedIn didn't emerge through happenstance. It was a series of intentional and deliberate decisions by ex-CEO, Jeff Weiner and current CEO, Ryan Roslansky. As their peer Mark Zuckerberg misfired again and again, they quietly built up the trust, momentum and resolve to grow a social media platform finally fit for modern-day purposes: creating economic opportunity for every member of the global workforce.

And this is why I have the utmost respect for LinkedIn, and Microsoft overall. I always express my admiration for Satya Nadella and believe the culture he's worked hard to build during his 8-year tenure as CEO has largely shaped the value system inherent within both Microsoft and LinkedIn. Don't get me wrong, they're both very different types of companies, but both operate with a fundamental respect and honour towards doing the right thing. Whether that's through the products that they build, the people that they hire or the way that they make operating decisions.

I believe we're on the brink of a brave new meta world. And as we find ourselves within the gaping chasm of this new meta world, we must pause and pay homage to the world we're leaving behind. The analogue and tactile world born out of physical connection and community. One in which we devoted the time and energy into developing real-world relationships. And as we're collectively expected to jump down the metaverse rabbit hole headfirst, digitizing every aspect of our livelihood – from finance to work to socialization – we should acknowledge, from as centrist a view as possible, what real risks will arise, and what the potential upside can be. As with any seismic change, the metaverse future is vast and undetermined. It must be moulded with careful and compassionate hands to create a universe where we collectively thrive and succeed.

Chapter 7: The Fall of Sense
Dona Varghese

"The real problem of humanity is the following: we have Palaeolithic emotions, medieval institutions and godlike technology."
- E. O Wilson

Technology makes art possible.

To Plato, art was the imitation of nature. But in the 19th century, photography took over that function, and in the 20th century, abstract art overturned the entire notion that art was about "representation".

So, what is art? There have been many attempts to define it, but this ambivalence makes it possible to look at art in many ways – as an imitator, as something that creates harmony or something that reveals the essential or hidden truth.

Art is everywhere – it has a way of making invisible things appear, it creates questions. And if art generates debate, technology is what makes it possible. Art can't exist without technology; artists have always depended on technology to innovate, and over the years technology has also changed the way we view art. Today, tech is redefining art in strange, new ways. Works can be created by people moving through laser beams or from the data gathered on air pollution.

Where would the Impressionists have been without the invention of portable paint tubes that enabled them to paint outdoors? Who would have heard of Andy Warhol without the invention of silkscreen printing? The truth is that technology has been providing artists with new ways to express themselves for a very long time.

Contemporary art has been greatly influenced by the rapid development in digital technology and by the astonishing progression in the introduction of new, more attractive, and tougher materials that artists can work with. Both these innovations have expanded the horizons of creativity and opened up new artistic frontiers. They've also allowed contemporary artists to reduce time spent in the actual execution of artwork to a minimum, thereby freeing them to focus more on ideation, creativity and developing ground-breaking work, including the integration of sound into a visual story.

As technology advances, choices multiply – new mediums lead to more options, modes of expression, and representation for underheard voices.

But this expanding landscape isn't without its downfalls. Choice overload is an acutely modern anxiety, growing larger with every new app we download. Let's face it, we have too many places from which to order food, too many people to swipe left or right on. And so we're always making poor decisions. It can't be helped. It's a malady inescapable even in the art world.

Galleries like American Medium work with young artists who are approaching web-based art with a renewed purpose. They cater to an audience that has grown up with the internet. Even when the digital components aren't obvious, the work exhibited in the gallery is often influenced by the internet. In "Lavendra," a show by artist E. Jane, images of '90s R&B YouTube videos are extracted and printed on fabric. E. Jane says the resolutions are lower than those found on old videos featuring white pop singers, simply because not many people cared to upload higher-quality versions. This bluntly reflects the limited staying power of black female artists in popular culture.

There was an exhibition in London called "Assemblance", and it was designed to encourage visitors to create light structures and floor drawings by moving through coloured laser beams and smoke. The shapes produced were fragile, especially when people worked alone. But those who collaborated discovered that the light structures they created were more resilient and more sophisticated. How cool is that?! Like building sandcastles on the beach, Assemblance explored how to structure participation to build trust between people, who must sometimes suspend disbelief in order to cooperate and co-exist. The space, at times magical, at times slightly sinister, created deep emotional engagement by blurring arbitrary distinctions between the physical and virtual.

Here's another perfect example of how technology is reshaping what art is and how it's produced – an immersive laser experience by artists Usman Haque and Dot Samsen, known for their large-scale mass participatory interactive events. An exhibition held at the Museum of Modern Art in New York called "New Order: Art and Technology in the Twenty-First Century," is a show of 25 works made since the turn of the millennium and drawn entirely from the museum's collection. People and connoisseurs from the world over support the claim that these pieces "push the boundaries of technology." This exhibition questions the role of art in our over-wired lives. in May 2018, David Hockney: Something New in Painting (and photography) [and even printing] exhibition at Pace Gallery, included 17 new paintings, the majority of which are painted on hexagonal canvases. The hexagonal canvases add a structural element to the artist's efforts to transcend the limitations of conventional perspective. The exhibition included works produced with the help of computer-manipulated photography and iPad software. Having always been interested in new media, these monumental prints are an exciting extension of Hockney's experimentation with reverse perspective into other media formats, beyond painting.

Rembrandt died in 1669, but a new piece of work created with computer data brings him back to life. Launched in the Netherlands, 'The Next Rembrandt' is a result of an 18-month project undertaken by a group of art historians, developers, scientists, engineers, and data geeks to recreate his style of painting. The result? Now almost any piece of art could be skinned in Rembrandt's style, allowing his legacy to live on. There is no doubt that artists are facing increasingly more complex and unprecedented challenges to presenting distinctive artwork in the face of the many recent technological advances that have expanded and diversified the art world. It's no surprise then that artists find it more challenging than ever to deliver original and innovative ideas, needing to exert themselves and truly stretch their imagination to succeed.

If art is representation, technology makes it possible. Is the natural evolution NFTs? You'd have to be living under a rock to not have heard of them, but their meaning, workings and purpose is still a hazy concept for most to just get on board with.

So, what are NFTs? NFT stands for "non-fungible token", which is just a term used to describe a unique digital media asset, whose ownership is tracked on a blockchain. The ownership could be for a broad range of digital goods like art, fashion and real estate, which may or may not have real-life, physical benefits attached to them as well. In simple terms, NFTs are a way to make digital files ownable – you can now own a JPEG or an MP3 of a basketball top shot meme. What's the point of this ownership? NFTs are tokenized assets that give investors many reasons to buy them. NFTs by themselves are not investments; its imperative one understands the value of the underlying asset. NFTs help anyone keep a track of ownership, its place of origin and attribution. Mainstream interest for NFTs has spread like wildfire – and these days one hears everything from "I've never seen anything like this before" to "is this like ICOs all over again?" to "it's just a jpg, I don't get it" to "but what about the energy use!"

All about Non-Fungible Tokens

The concept of NFTs is pretty broad. The crypto space is what made enabled NFTs to begin with, and in turn, blockchain is what enabled the crypto space. Let's use an analogy to delve deeper. Imagine a piece of art you created. Now, to protect and promote this piece of art you can record all the proof of your art in a book on the internet in a virtual register, which creates a unique identification card for your art. This virtual register is called Blockchain, where they use a special type of "ink". Investopedia defines blockchain as a distributed database that is shared among the nodes of a computer network. As a database, a blockchain stores information electronically in digital format. Blockchains are best known for their crucial role in cryptocurrency systems, such as Bitcoin, for maintaining a secure and decentralized record of transactions. The innovation with a blockchain is that it guarantees the fidelity and security of a record of data and generates trust without the need for a trusted third party. Basically, anyone can use this ink to write in the Blockchain, but nobody can delete anything. To find your art easily, a number is added. And voila! All your art information in the blockchain is called a token. Non-Fungible Tokens are unique and cannot be replaced. Meanwhile, something that is fungible can be easily replaced for another identical thing. For instance, you can exchange a $100 note for another $100 note. But you can't do the same with your art, because it's a unique piece that cannot be replaced by another piece of art. Simply put, a Non-Fungible Token is a tool that validates the private property of a digital asset. So, in our example, you are the owner of your artwork, and NFT proves it. Today, the majority of NFTs are digital, which makes it very easy for creators to give their supporters something unique and rare. While they are like Bitcoins and other cryptocurrencies, they are non-fungible and non-divisible.

To fully understand NFTs, it's important to note some of the properties of Blockchain, namely: security, stability, scalability, supply, decentralization, demand and use case. The blockchain is good at tracking the history of things, and the use of NFTs and smart contracts enables cutting out the middlemen and the costs that come along with them.

It's worth mentioning some of the headlines that generated awareness and curiosity about NFTs. Beeple (real name is Mike Winkelmann) sells NFT for $69 million. Twitter CEO Jack Dorsey's first tweet sells for $2.9 million. Digital home sells for $500,000 in the latest NFT sale. Burnt Banksy sells for $380,000. That's just to name a few. WhaleShark – a British, Hong Kong-based collector – began putting at least half his salary into Bitcoin as early as 2012, then in 2015 switched to Ether. "I think the main reason why NFTs started to blow up is that people started to realize it's just a natural evolution," he says. "Our life is slowly turning from physical to digital. When you look at the younger generation, they are very accustomed to holding digital collectibles as a store of value." A handful of collectors already have millions of dollars' worth.

It sounds like everything could be an NFT. Well guess what? Anything in the world can be an NFT! If you create something unique that can be owned – it can easily be converted into an NFT. So, what is an NFT and what isn't? NFTs exist in both the physical and digital world. For instance, the Mona Lisa by Leonardo da Vinci, currently owned by French Republic, is non-fungible and the only of its kind, it can be duplicated but there is only one Mona Lisa by Leonardo da Vinci. This would make Mona Lisa by Leonardo da Vinci an NFT Art would. Blockchain has enabled digital NFTs to flourish. Today, NFTs are super powerful, because they allow anyone to issue, own and trade them. What makes them even more interesting is that they are borderless, making assets significantly easier to transfer. This wouldn't be the case if the French Republic wanted to transfer ownership of the Mona Lisa to, let's say, a prominent art collector in America. The trouble with physical goods is that they are in custody with someone, and the process to transfer would require multiple steps like audit, paperwork, country-to-country law, etc. In the digital world, this whole process is decentralized. Additionally, NFT activity goes beyond trading and includes actions and activities like being able to borrow and lend, support fractional ownership, or possibly use NFTs as collateral to take out loans. The possibilities are endless! For example, the game Aavegotchi combines DeFi and NFT gaming, whereby each Aavegotchi character represents a user's collateral that is deposited within the lending platform Aave, but you can also battle the characters, level them up, and equip wearables that change their traits.

NFTs include a wide range of areas, given they are simply digital proof of ownership. And so far, the most significant growth has been within art and gaming. Note that many digital works of art and gaming items are a subset of a larger category of NFT collectibles.

Another emerging space includes social tokens – which are in the NFT category, or at the very least, closely related to it. So, what are social tokens? They're a broad category of tokens introduced and issued by individuals and communities. Social tokens are also called personal tokens, community tokens and creator tokens. What they do is just enable creators and communities to have more ownership in things they are building. They tend to get lumped together because both NFTs and social tokens promote the creator community, helping them to engage with their audience over and above ownership proof. But the bottom line is that if its fungible – it's not an NFT.

Matt Levine on Twitter said "NFTs are a new form of tradable ostentation rather than a new form of tradable ownership." Maybe it is, but it's important to note that there are many use cases of NFTs – it's an efficient way of transferring ownership without having as much paperwork and middlemen involved.

I'm optimistic that we are going to experience a huge wave of creativity and experimentation in the NFT space. It's an exciting time to see the boom of a creators' economy and what one can own today! That being said, I'm equally sceptical about a huge wave of digital hacking, terrorism and decentralized catastrophic power.

Crypto & Why Crypto Scams are driving an online crime boom?

Crypto networks are unique because of their potential to scale exponentially. The essence of crypto networks is their ability to grow network effects (a phenomenon whereby a product or service gains additional value as more people use it) by enabling users to share in the value they create. That said, many individuals claim that crypto projects don't capture value, as they are based on open-source code. Basically, anyone can come along, copy the codes and lure investors away to another platform. It's that simple! Like the internet we know and understand today, a well-designed crypto network is a live, always- on running service that allows users to enjoy the strong network effects, while equally running the risk of being easily copied (or forked). For instance, Bitcoin's network effect derives from more people considering it a store of value, which in turn, incentivizes miners to secure the network. Ethereum's network effect derives from developers who deploy apps – each becomes a building block that other developers can compose into higher-order services, driving increased usage, and demand for ETH. But without trust and familiarity (brand equity), smart contract integration, network effects, switching costs and the Lindy effect[1], cryptocurrencies could not be successful.

Crypto networks like Bitcoin and Ethereum are the very first community-owned-and-operated platforms at scale. Today, many more founders have

1 The Lindy effect (also known as Lindy's Law) is a theorized phenomenon by which the future life expectancy of some non-perishable things, like a technology or an idea, is proportional to their current age. Thus, the Lindy effect proposes the longer a period something has survived to exist or be used in the present, it is also likely to have a longer remaining life expectancy. Longevity implies a resistance to change, obsolescence or competition, and greater odds of continued existence into the future. Where the Lindy effect applies, mortality rate decreases with time. Mathematically, the Lindy effect corresponds to lifetimes, following Pareto probability distribution.

The concept is named after Lindy's delicatessen in New York City, where the idea was informally theorized by comedians. The Lindy effect has subsequently been theorized by mathematicians and statisticians. Nassim Nicholas Taleb has expressed the Lindy effect in terms of "distance from an Absorbing barrier."

been able to leverage this new stack as a tool to distribute economic value, build network effects and generate value for themselves, investors, and their user communities. Some bad players have leveraged this too.

Crypto scams are on the rise, and online crimes are only going up. The crypto playground is vast, accessible, and lush with opportunities to take advantage. And the worst part is that these scams are tapping into human vulnerability to create negative change in their lives.

An article published in TIME magazine on March 29, 2022, called "Why Crypto Scams Are Driving an Online Crime Boom — And How to Outsmart Them" highlights a heart-breaking crypto romance story that cost the victim $306,000 and trust issues. Two people met on an online dating app, started their romance, and shared the most intimate moments – virtually. They exchanged their deepest desires and goals for their future, and planned to build a family. To fund their dreams, the scamster encouraged his partner to start investing in Bitcoin through Coinbase. Both established platforms. Now the twist occurred much later. The scamster advised to transfer the funds to his preferred platforms while consistently reassuring his partner – "babe, we are doing this for our future". It was not until the investing partner tried to withdraw her gains did she realize that this man was a con artist and she had been transferring the funds straight to professional crooks. This is just one of many such incidents that have occurred over the last couple of years.

According to Io Dodds, a freelance reporter for TIME Magazine, "Cryptocurrency scams are driving an online crime boom right now. Romance scams, investment scams, digital wallet hacks, pyramid schemes, ransomware attacks, and even digital art thefts – the methods may be different, but wherever you find a cybercrime victim, odds are good that crypto was involved."

In a report from the research firm Chainalysis, which tracks the movement of cryptocurrency across the internet, $14 billion worth of cryptocurrencies was sent to "illicit" wallet addresses in 2020, triple the amount for 2017. Those digital wallets may have been used for fraud, terrorism, or payments for child abuse material. There are so many crypto- romance victims – they've actually formed an advocacy group, the Global Anti-Scam Organization (GASO). In 2021 alone, GASO's fraud reports added up to $73 million in losses.

There are many challenges of recovering money in crypto scams – and with no central resource for credible crypto-related information and no legal recourse in the absence of regulations, investors attract scamsters and hackers waiting to trap gullible investors.

The uncontrollable issue with these websites is the number of them on the internet. If one is taken down, like whack-a-mole, another one pops up to take its place. To make things worse, these scamsters also use varying modus operandi. They can dupe investors through email scams, phishing scams, giveaway scams – and that is just scratching the surface of the different tricks they have up their sleeves.

On February 26, 2022, Twitter accounts that belonged to the Ukrainian Government posted pleas for crypto asset donation. Crypto's role in the Ukraine Crisis is another great example of decentralized power. Following Russia's invasion of Ukraine, the Ukrainian government solicited donations in cryptocurrency – making this the first time ever a nation accepted financial support through decentralized methods! What followed, of course, was tens of millions raised in donations by the Ukrainian government and NGOs in Bitcoin, Ethereum, stable coins and NFTs. To add to these, suppliers of the Ukrainian government even started accepting crypto as payment. So, what does it mean when Ukraine Government turns to Crypto to crowdfund millions of dollars?

According to Elliptic (provides blockchain analytics for crypto assets compliance), as of March 11, 2022, the Ukrainian Government and Come Back Alive NGO (provides support to the military) have raised over $63.8 million, through more than 120,000 crypto asset donations since the start of the Russian invasion. The donations included a single transaction worth $1.86 million, which came from the sale of NFTs created by Julian Assange and the digital artist Pak. A CryptoPunk NFT worth approximately $200,000 was sent to the Ukrainian government's Ethereum account.

Scammers also appear to be taking advantage of the current situation by tricking unsuspecting users wishing to donate to Ukrainian causes. Elliptic has identified several fraudulent crypto fundraising scams which are exploiting the current situation.

Will crypto donations continue to be meaningful, or will scammers take over? Who is responsible for educating investors to make well-informed investment decisions and practice due diligence when trading in crypto, or any other form of investment? Are we on the fast lane to Decentralized Catastrophic power?

Ok, let's backtrack just a bit. What is decentralization? According to Oxford Dictionary, decentralization is the transfer of control of an activity or organization to several local offices or authorities rather than one single one. Decentralization in blockchain refers to the transfer of control and decision-making from a centralized entity. The idea is that decentralized networks strive to reduce the level of trust that participants must place in one another and deter their ability to exert authority or control over one another, in ways that degrade the functionality of the network. While blockchain technologies often make use of decentralized networks, a blockchain application itself cannot be categorized simply as being decentralized or not.

Let's take a moment to understand different types of systems, outlined in the table below:

Comparison Points	Centralized	Distributed	Decentralized
Network/hardware resources	Maintained and controlled by a single entity in a single location.	Spread across multiple data centres and geographies, owned by a network provider.	Resources are owned and shared by network members; difficult to maintain since no single owner.
Solutions component	Maintained and controlled by central entity.	Maintained and controlled by solution provider.	Each member has the same copy of distributed ledger.
Data	Maintained and controlled by a central entity.	Typically owned and managed by the customer.	Only added through group consensus.
Control	Controlled by a central entity.	Typically, a shared responsibility between network provider, solution provider and customer.	No one owns the data, and everyone owns the data.
Single Point of Failure	Yes	No	No
Fault Tolerance	Low	High	Extremely high
Security	Maintained and controlled by a central entity.	Typically, a shared responsibility between the network provider, solution provider and the customer.	Increases as the number of members increases.
Performance	Maintained and controlled by a central entity.	Increases as network/hardware resources scale up and out.	Decreases as the number of members increases.
Example	ERP System	Cloud Computing	Blockchain

Here's a deep point to think about in regards to the state of the world – one of the things about exponential technology means the more exponentially powerful the technology, the more exponentially cheaper it will become – which also means that it's going to be more distributed. Soon this level of technology will not only get better, but will also be more easily available for people to use as they please. But what happens when you have an internet where not only do you have decentralized finance and AI curating social media feeds – but also have AI creating content, and thereby maximizing its toxicity?

Tristan Harris calls it "God-like Technology". Why? Because it inherently has decentralized catastrophic capabilities. So how do we make it through having decentralized exponential technology? And deeper still – between polarization, affective polarization, persuasion tactics implemented by social media platforms, decentralized finance and AI curating and creating content and programs – how do marketers and technology ethically influence individuals?

Metacrisis

Edward O. Wilson, the Harvard professor and renowned father of socio-biology said over a decade ago, "The real problem of humanity is the following: we have Palaeolithic emotions, medieval institutions and godlike technology." Since the launch of the first social media platform in 1997 (Six Degrees, founded by Andrew Weinreich) our technological evolution grew exponentially – but can we say the same about human reactions and impulses? Our natural impulse, even today, is to raise our concerns about tech companies collecting and mining our personal data, as opposed to how this exponential growth has overwhelmed the natural capacities of our brains. But at the same time, our natural instincts can't resist the temptation to experience technology's deep temptations. Every interstitial moment of our internet lives is out there to be consumed, engaged with, shared and validated. Data is the currency we pay in to participate in the online world. Yet this participation means compromised privacy, along with unfavourable impacts on our mental health. This omnipresent awareness of the world is actually having a deep impact on our brains. We live in a world of hyper-personalized newsfeeds, where no two individuals are consuming the same information – information that confirms our beliefs and makes us feel accepted, or information that challenges our belief system and makes us feel alone and helpless. Simply put, technological advancement doesn't match our evolutionary advancement – leading to issues like misinformation, disinformation, affective polarization, deepfake, depression, anxiety... the list goes on. Technological advancement is directly proportional to the downgrading of humanity.

Today, humanity is in metacrisis mode, enabled by technology. And these issues are growing more and more complex each day. But a well-stated problem is half solved. How is the meta crisis impacting our lives? What is the metacrisis? What are the patterns of human behaviour as we increase our technological capabilities? Is it increasing catastrophic risk as opposed to increasing advantageous solutions? What's really driving global problems in the world today? How is the interconnected nature of the many crises we're facing as a society (climate change, inequality, etc.) impacting our creative energy to solve these problems?

According to Jonathan Rowson (co-founder of Perspectiva), "Meta means many things. In its simplest definition, it means after. But it's sometimes used to mean between. It's sometimes used to mean within. It seems to change its meaning slightly, depending on what it's describing. It has a chameleon quality in that way. So, the first thing about meta is to realize it means many things. You could say the metacrisis is the crisis of perception and understanding that lies within the range of crises humanity faces."

According to Terry Patten (philosopher, author, activist, and social entrepreneur), "The metacrisis is a single phenomenon. We may be thinking of it as an ecological crisis. We may be thinking of it as a psychological or spiritual crisis. We may be thinking of it as a cultural crisis and a breakdown of community, family, etc. We may be thinking of it as a crisis of government and economics and finance. And it is all these things. But it's not reducible to any one of them. That's why it's a metacrisis."

What are some of the crises?

- Covid Reckoning
- Climate Emergency
- Societal Crisis
- Socio-emotional Crisis
- Educational Crisis
- Epistemic Crisis
- Spiritual Crisis
- Corporate Management Crisis
- Centralized System Crisis
- Decentralized System Crisis
- Authoritarianism Crisis
- Meme Culture Crisis

"In addition to these challenges, we have the underlying crisis in governance, which includes things like what to do with pervasive inequality, and how do you redesign the economy so that it's no longer about indefinite economic growth? And then it's also about the emergency. What do you do about incipient climate collapse? These things are all happening at the same time. They're all part of one predicament that we need to somehow feel our way into and grow into so that we can become what we must become to deal with these challenges of our time."

Metacrisis in the context of technology is the compounding effect of the complexities of all issues – climate change is complex, nuclear power is complex, social media is complex, GPT-3 issue is complex, CRISPR biotech is complex, etc. Our complexities are growing exponentially, but our capacity to deal with these issues is growing logarithmically and advancing very slowly. Now factor in social media, and you polarize people and divide them into personalized versions of reality. In fact, social media rewards the most cynical take on anything. When a cynical take on things goes viral, we lose trust in so much. Social media isn't trying to polarize the population – extremity is a side effect. The trouble with having an open technology and platforms (not regulated for human mental capabilities and capacity) is that people come along and put things there. It's like when someone puts a dumpster on the side of the road because they're moving houses and want to get rid of all the junk they've accumulated over the years. The next thing you know, the whole neighbourhood's thrown their junk in and the dumpster's full.

There were two landmark dystopian novels written by brilliant British cultural critics – Brave New World by Aldous Huxley and Nineteen Eighty-Four by George Orwell – and we have mistakenly feared and obsessed over the vision portrayed in the latter book (an information-censoring, movement-restricting, individuality-emaciating state) rather than the former (a technology-sedating, consumption-engorging, instant-gratifying bubble). Today we are living in a polarized world: centralized tech vs decentralized tech, religion-based politics vs secular politics, attention economy vs abstinence economy. What enabled this world? Technology! Technology that makes us more distracted, divided, and confused reduces our ability to react wisely. And technology that gives us God-like powers increases the need to act wisely.

If we take China as an example, where technological algorithms are derived for social monitoring and not built on advertising models like the rest of the world, you will notice how their relationship and usage differ from the typical global standard. If you ask China who they think is the greatest threat to their society, you would automatically think their answer would be America. In actually, they consider technology to be the greatest threat to society. Some of the steps China has taken to protect her society are from a technological point of view. For instance, scrolling uses mandatory delays to discourage mindless scrolling behaviour, children under the age of 14 have time limitations and newsfeeds show content around science, education, and patriotism. They are using TikTok to educate their children to grow up wanting to be astronauts and scientists instead of influencers. And their TikTok usage is limited to 40 mins a day! By contrast, open societies, Western societies and democracies are not consciously saying "let's use technology to advance humanity instead of advancing consumerism". If we take the Chinese Communist Party model as an example, they are using technology for their ideological goals – whereas in the big tech corporation model they are using it purely for profit.

So, the real conundrum here is how to ethically influence people. How do we work this out? How is persuasive technology being used to harvest time and attention? Technology is the pen writing human history. And now that we have dozens of potentially catastrophic weapons in the form of technology, we are in an unprecedented time of risk.

There was recently a TikTok challenge that's emboldened and popularized a destructive trend, called "devious licks". This challenge encouraged kids to take videos of themselves destroying school bathrooms. The virality nature of social media platforms actually enabled vandalizing behaviour among young kids! This challenge was later removed, but this is just one of the many examples of how unethical persuasion is occurring on social media. It's not even the first time a social media trend has proven destructive. Several years ago, a viral video led to a rash of poisonings, encouraging teenagers to swallow pods of laundry detergent for the "Tide Pods challenge." And another huge issue – gun violence influenced by social media. Innocent children getting shot because of social media posts, and rumors around posts. As hard as it can be to be disappointed in our children, it's worth trying to listen deeper and seeing if these issues have a durable solution.

When it comes to the power of technology, this is a really important gut check for all of us. The truth of the matter is that bad actors exist no matter what. We are going to swing back and forth based on the purpose technology is used for. For instance, when the internet came out it was very powerful for a bunch of bad actors, but we can't lose sight of how many positively powerful ways it was used for as well. If it's negative – we call for regulation. If it's positive, we call for scaling the good exponentially.

Technology is so mighty that its impact for good can have infinite potential. We can't let some bad apples detract us from that. It's virtually impossible to create technology that is used only for good and never for bad – we must look at this from a place of balance.

A narrow solution by Facebook whistle-blower Frances Haugen called out for urgent external regulation. She asked Facebook to remove their re-share button. According to Frances, there have been internal studies done by Facebook suggesting that if the re-share button were removed, after two shares, this small frictionless change could have exponential impact in the spread of misinformation, disinformation, and polarization. What this means is that if something is truly that meaningful, you will post it on your own, counter to the influencer and virality culture that the re-share button currently enables. Actually, this could possibly lead to the end of the meme-pandemic! This model of social media is not intended to create polarization, but that's just the by-product of social media. These attention and virality modes are unfortunately leading to a polarization of the population, dividing the representative class, and creating more gridlocks in thoughts and actions – which leads to the crumbling of the economy.

Some tech platforms are taking steps to curb negative impacts. Facebook alone deletes up to 2 billion fake accounts on a quarterly basis – a process known as the Information Quality Report. Information Quality is an approach that has helped researchers evaluate the quality of information output, including social media. It aims to address the problem of sharing misinformation online and evaluates the impact of Facebook's fact-checking approach on the quality metrics within the Information Quality field. It's not all bad! But we are still a long way from home free.

There's a new version of AI technology that has the capability of generating information. It's a tool called GPT-3, and it's also known as the Generative Pre-trained Transformer 3. GPT-3 is an autoregressive language model that uses deep learning to produce human-like text. Mario Klingemann, an artist who works with machine learning, shared a short story called "The importance of being on Twitter," written in the style of Jerome K. Jerome, which starts: "It is a curious fact that the last remaining form of social life in which the people of London are still interested is Twitter. I was struck with this curious fact when I went on one of my periodical holidays to the seaside and found the whole place twittering like a starling-cage." Klingemann says all he gave the AI was the title, the author's name and the initial "It." There is even a reasonably informative article about GPT-3 – written entirely by GPT-3. Yet despite its new tricks, GPT-3 is still prone to spewing hateful sexist and racist language. This is where the issue occurs. How do we navigate through this hot mess?

Some questions I asked Open AI's GPT-3 playground for study notes:

Dona Varghese: Is the world doomed?
GPT-3: There is no definitive answer, but some people believe that the world is doomed because of the way humans are impacting the environment.

Dona Varghese: Is God real?
GPT-3: There is no one answer to this question as people have different beliefs. Some people believe that there is a god or gods who created and control the universe, while others believe that there is no god.

Dona Varghese: Is covid-19 a biotech virus?
GPT-3: There is no evidence that COVID-19 is a bio-engineered virus.

Another god-like technology called CRISPR could prove to be a massive threat to humanity. What is CRISPR? CRISPR is a technology for changing the DNA sequence in cells in a precise fashion to correct mutations that otherwise cause disease. How does it work? By the action of a protein called Cas9 that functions like a molecular cousin for DNA. The CRISPR Cas9 system has an amazing ability to recognize a particular DNA sequence in a cell that may be non-functioning, and disable it by cutting the DNA. This is what's called gene editing. It can be used to disable or repair a mutated part of a gene, which might be causing disease. For Cas9 to find the malfunctioning DNA, we attach it to an RNA sequence that matches the DNA sequence we want to edit, then we put this RNA Cas9 combination to the cell to find the mutant DNA, and using a chemical reaction, the DNA strand is cut right at the spot where it's malfunctioning. After that, we can sometimes insert the correct version of the gene for the cell to work properly again. Fascinating! This is a very exciting technology that is going to do a lot of good in human society and for human health. It stretches from human therapeutics to agricultural applications to thinking about how we make better biofuels. But this also begs the question: how would bad actors use this for manipulative purposes?

CRISPR reminds me of this Sci-Fri movie called Gattaca, where the doctor says "You want your child to have the best possible start, believe me, we have enough imperfections built-in already. Your child doesn't need any additional burdens." CRISPR is a pair of molecular scissors currently being tested on cells that impact cancer, lymphoma, sickle cell anaemia and childhood blindness. There is evidence of CRISPR being used make cells resistant to HIV. Who wouldn't want their child to be free of avoidable burdens? Now the more important question is – who has the means to think like this? What are the ethics behind creating designer babies? Proponents of genetic editing say it could eliminate disease, reduce medical costs and spare people from suffering. That kind of thinking scares the hell out of me. Are we creating a world of economic disparity? Over and above what we experience already? Is perfection the golden ticket or a burden? In the process of precise gene editing, would it be possible to eliminate heartbreak and disappointment?

We are the one species that can act first instead of waiting for disaster to happen. We have the capacity to understand that our technological advancement is not in alignment with human advancement. Humans as individuals and humankind will increasingly have to deal with things nobody ever encountered before, such as super-intelligent machines, engineered bodies, algorithms that can manipulate our emotions with uncanny precision, rapid man-made climate cataclysms, and the need to change our profession every decade. (Harari, Y. N. N. (2019). 21 Lessons for the 21st Century (Reprint ed.). Random House Publishing Group.)

How does one navigate through life when they're flooded with enormous amounts of information – without enough time or capacity to absorb and analyse it? Digital Detox, Digital Abstinence, and Connecting with Values aren't unfamiliar terms to us these days. To survive and flourish in the metaverse one requires a lot of mental flexibility and great reserves of emotional balance. Less mental clutter means more mental resources available for deep thinking. (Newport, C. (2022). Deep Work. Platkus Books.)

Technology isn't bad if we know what we want in life. In fact, technology can help us get there, when accessed with clarity. Today, if you take a moment to notice you will see everyone is looking at the device in their palms. Do you think they control the technology, or does the technology control them? If technology is in control of your life, perhaps it's not too crazy to think that it can propel dangerous feedback loops.

Is World War III really a War of Information? If yes, when did it start?

I used Open AI's GPT-3 playground for study notes, where I asked what are the five things I must know about information war?

The GPT-3 broke it down into within seconds:

Dona Varghese: What is information warfare?
GPT-3: Information warfare is the use of information technology to attack an opponent's computer systems and networks in order to disrupt, disable, or destroy their information and communications infrastructure.

Dona Varghese: What are the goals of information warfare?
GPT-3: The goals of information warfare are to deny, degrade, and disrupt the enemy's ability to use information and information systems.

Dona Varghese: What are the methods of information warfare?
GPT-3: The methods of information warfare include but are not limited to: -Cyber-attacks -Disinformation campaigns -Hacking -Identity theft -Intelligence gathering -Phishing -Spamming -Virus and malware attacks.

Dona Varghese: What are the benefits of information warfare?
GPT-3 Some benefits of information warfare include being able to gather intelligence on an enemy, being able to disrupt an enemy's communications, and being able to disable an enemy's computer systems.

Dona Varghese: What are the risks of information warfare? GPT-3: The risks of information warfare include the following:

- Data breaches and cyber-attacks: A data breach is when an unauthorized individual gains access to sensitive information. This can happen when a hacker breaks into a computer system or when an employee accidentally leaks information. A cyber-attack is when a hacker deliberately tries to disrupt a computer system or steal information.
- Disruption of critical infrastructure: Information warfare can be used to disrupt critical infrastructure, such as power grids or communication networks. This can cause widespread blackouts or communication breakdowns.
- Manipulation of information: Information warfare can be used to manipulate public opinion by spreading false information or by censoring the truth. This can lead to social unrest or even violence.
- Economic damage: Information warfare can be used to damage a country's economy by sabotaging financial markets or stealing trade secrets.

• Escalation of conflict: Information warfare can be used to escalate a conflict between two countries. This can lead to a real-world war.

The Russian-Ukraine War

Two former republics of the Soviet Union are in conflict, once again. The history of tension goes back as a long as a century, perhaps more. In 1918, Ukraine declared independence from Russia during a conflict fought by multiple countries and armies over several years. Its independence and sovereignty received international recognition at the Treaty of Brest-Litovsk. In 1921, the Ukrainian Soviet Socialist Republic was founded, and Ukraine was subsumed into the Soviet Union the following year. A century later, in 2021-2022, President Vladimir V. Putin of Russia started seeking to prevent Ukraine's drift toward the United States and its allies. Mr. Putin demanded "security guarantees," including an assurance by NATO that Ukraine will never join the group and that the alliance pulls back troops stationed in countries that joined after 1997. (A history of the tensions between Ukraine and Russia. (2022, March 26). Matthew Mpoke Bigg. www.nytimes.com)

How are we verifying the reporting on the Ukraine War? If social media algorithms are optimized for virality and hyper-personalized for users, what war reporting are you seeing vs mine? Would the impact of the most recent war become an example of information warfare? Are we verifying images of the war in Ukraine? And how is the marketing industry responding to this war?

The free flow of information within and between nation states is essential to business, international relations, and social cohesion, as much as information is essential to a military force's ability to fight. Communications today lean heavily on the internet, or on social media platforms like Facebook, Twitter, Instagram, TikTok, or Clubhouse – just to name a few. Twitter published a blog (March 16, 2022) on their official site that addressed their ongoing approach to the war in Ukraine. Twitter's key priority was to keep people on Twitter safe by actively monitoring risks associated with the conflicts in Ukraine – including identifying and disrupting attempts to amplify false and misleading information. Twitter paused advertising in Ukraine and Russia to ensure critical public safety information is elevated and ads don't detract from it. They assured their users that as the situations evolves, they would take the necessary steps to combat potential harm and surface reliable information. According to Statista Research Department (as of December 2020), Twitter, a microblogging company, employs 5,500 people around the world. But it still remains to be seen just how efficiently social media platforms match their good intentions with actions.

If you browse through Ukraine's Twitter account, the world is processing trauma – in real-time. TikToks of cats in cardboard tanks. Flirty comments on Instagram accounts dedicated to Vladmir Putin, begging him to stop Russia's attacks on Ukraine. Memes bemoaning what it's like to live during a pandemic followed by war. In chapter 3, I encouraged you to examine Marshal McLuhan's phrase – The medium is the message – and presented the argument that changes in modes of communication have an important effect on the trajectory of social evolution and the values and beliefs of societies. And if that's the case, then Russia's invasion of Ukraine reveals that memes and cute cat content are no longer just for fun and entertainment. Now, the cultural practices underscoring internet culture have become a framework through which we process catastrophe. If the medium is the message, then internet cultural practices have become intertwined with geopolitical and military conflicts.

How is the marketing industry responding to the Ukraine War?

A significant impact was in fact created by the crypto world, raising awareness and collecting contributions through crypto.com, which was supporting Ukraine with NFT collections called "Meta History: Museum of War".

The museum records the timeline of Russia's invasion and channels proceeds to Ukraine's army and civilians. Brands like Microsoft declared they would redirect a certain section of proceeds made from their popular online game Fortnite to aid Ukraine. Meta CEO Mark Zuckerberg called Russia's invasion of Ukraine a "massively destabilizing world event" and approved to block Russian state-backed media accounts in Ukraine and the European Union. Russia, in turn, responded by blocking Facebook and Instagram. A few Pharma companies stopped operations in Russia. Airbnb secured housing for Ukrainian refugees. Publicis & IPG are a few of the latest media companies to suspend their operations, engagement, and investment in Russia due to the ongoing invasion of Ukraine. Burger King pulled support, Heineken and Molson Coors paused Russian activity. As of March 10, 2022 Goldman Sachs declared the intention to exit Russia. Market Research platforms like Kantar & Neilson talked about suspending activities. Amazon stopped sending products to Russia; cut off Prime Video. Google suspended advertising in Russia. The list goes on…

"Beyond the commercial world, many don't understand just how complicated the situation is for some big brands." - Mark Borkowski, crisis PR consultant and author. For brand leaders, what is the cost of staying in Russia vs the cost of leaving? No doubt brands have been quick to react to this Russian Evil. Who are we punishing here? Putin or everyday Russians? What about the brands who continued to do business? Is failure to exit Russia seen as an endorsement of evil?

Misinformation, Disinformation & Affective Polarization

The narrative about anything today is disseminated online and the verification process begins after it's out there –rarely before and mostly after it goes out. Content creation and consumption is decentralized. What does that mean? Simply put, it's a form of content creation and distribution that eliminates intermediaries that regulate and monitor before production and consumption. Its only after the propaganda is out there that moderators and regulators can do anything about it! Russia's involvement goes as deep as the American Elections, Arab Spring, Sri Lanka religious riots, Religion dominated politics in India, Covid-19 – and so on.

In the online world, no matter what your thoughts or questions, you will find enough evidence to validate these thoughts and echo them back to you. Is the world really flat? Sure, Google gave me about 5,04,00,00,000 results in 0.45 seconds to validate my thought and answer my question. Is Covid a bio tech engineered virus? Google presented about 6,61,00,000 results in 0.63 seconds, most of which, no doubt, say "yes". As humans, are we the cause of our reality today or are we living in the effects of it? What are the consequences of fake news? And how about deepfakes in the metaverse? We are all part of confirmation bias and filter bubbles.

A great example to truly understand misinformation, disinformation and affective polarization is the existence of QAnon. QAnon is a political conspiracy theory that later evolved into a political movement. It originated in the American far-right political sphere. QAnon centres on false claims made by an anonymous individual or individuals known as "Q". They claim that a cabal of Satanic, cannibalistic sexual abusers of children operating a global child sex trafficking ring conspired against former U.S. President Donald Trump during his term in office. Some experts have described QAnon as a cult. QAnon has infiltrated each platform based on their audience's relationship with their preferred platform. This enables a sense of native messaging that distracts the audience from asking if this information was fact checked. As a digital media marketing expert, I have spent hours in client boardrooms emphasizing on tweaking content and creative work based on the platform selected. How we talk to our brand's audience on Twitter differs from how we talk to them on Instagram, Facebook, Discord, or WhatsApp. We tweak content based on the platform interface.

Analogies I still use today go as follows. With Google search, your audience is looking for you, bidding on as many relevant keywords as possible to ensure you appear when they look for the brand. Facebook is your scrapbook, and mostly limited to the people you know. Instagram is the public history of your private life – for anyone who wants to access it. Twitter is your interest-based platform – type in a keyword and watch it evolve. Clubhouse is your real-time podcast. TikTok is your instant gratification and short form history of people's private life.

QAnon implemented a similar logic when they started their campaign on Instagram. They used an inviting, soft color palate that Instagram audiences immediately responded to and started to replicate in infinite ways. QAnon started #savethechildren, which evolved into something so far away from the truth that the truth no longer mattered. #Savethechildren influenced celebrities to re-post fake content without taking a moment to verify who is in charge or the source of the information. You can see how dangerous it could be to have an influencer/brand ambassador posting something fake to millions of followers. My 86-old grandmother, who barely speaks English, called me up the other day to share a "fact" (fake) that claims drinking apple, beetroot and carrot juice will cure cancer. I asked her "Ammachi, what is the source of this information?" She responded sincerely, "Ah mole Facebook told me so."

What is the psychological impact of fake information? If we have Paleolithic emotions and an enormous overload of information, how are we differentiating between what's real and what's fake? Fake news is not new, but technology has increased it beyond human capacity. According to ancient Chinese military strategist Sun Tzu in The Art of War (written in 5th century BC), "All warfare is based on deception." We are living in a deceptive world where we don't need big guns to hurt people and economies – a post, a tweet, or an AI generated image will do! Breaking news is breaking us.

A problem is half solved if we know what we are solving.

The complexities of human problems are rising at exponential levels but human capacity to handle these complexities is almost negligible. The ability to regulate anything is being broken and shattered because the incendiary controversial take on everything goes viral! Tristan Harris asks, "How do we reverse-engineer this bad trip we have been on for the last 10 years? It's like a psychedelic trip where we have all fractured into this different reality, where we exist in the controversial interpretation of everything."

Tristan Harris is a pioneer when it comes to the quest for solving humanity's tech-induced problems. He started the Center for Humane Technology, previously known as Time Well Spent — a not-for-profit organization dedicated to radically reimagining the digital infrastructure. Its mission is to drive a comprehensive shift towards humane technology that supports collective well-being, democracy, and the shared information environment. Tristan Harris and the Center for Humane Technology are the kind of people and programs that should go viral!

Apple is one of the first tech companies to address the issues around Data Privacy and to challenge the advertising world with its data privacy and tracking features. Their mission is, refreshingly, to improve transparency and empower their users. Since 2020, their ad campaigns focus on raising awareness about the importance of protecting people's personal information online. Apple is commemorating Data Privacy Day (January 28) by sharing "A Day in the Life of Your Data," an easy- to-understand report illustrating how companies track user data across websites and apps.

According to Tristan Harris & Daniel Schmatchenberger, "Having a grasp on the magnitude of the challenge is an important starting point."

Individuals are responsible and accountable for their mental well-being just as much as the outside players — be it brands, politicians, or institutions. Together, our collective individual actions can handle the growing need for a change of system.

Here are some personal steps I have taken over the years to be the cause of my life and not the effect:

- I turned off my notifications.
- I removed toxic apps.
- I downloaded helpful apps after deep research, thought and analysis.

- I eliminated outrage from my cultural environment.
- I embrace challenges of opposing views with the same excitement I embrace validating views.
- I practice compassion.
- I've set boundaries in terms of screen time.
- I don't fill every interstitial moment of my life with something to do. I practice the art of doing nothing, deeply.
- I support journalism by paying for a subscription. This way I am a customer and not a product.

Our consumption habits are deeply influenced by our culture but as individuals, we have the internal power to be the change we want to see in this world.

Chapter 8: Unified Connectivity
Dona Varghese

"Saving on expenses may be an upside of tech innovation and investment, but the real goal should be creating value."
- John McManus

American Marketing Association's defines *Marketing* as the activity, set of institutions, and processes for creating, communicating, delivering, and exchanging offerings that have value for customers, clients, partners, and society at large. Digital Marketing defines activities executed via internet and digital technologies. Philip Kolter, influential business thinker and aptly dubbed "the Father of Modern Marketing" believes Traditional and Digital Marketing must be wholly integrated.

Digital Marketing is not meant to replace Traditional Marketing. Instead, the two should coexist with interchanging roles across the consumer's path. In the early stage of interaction between companies and consumers, traditional marketing plays a major role in building awareness and interest. As the interaction progresses and the customer demands closer relationships with companies, digital marketing in turn rises in importance. The most important role of digital marketing is to drive action and brand advocacy[2]. Since digital marketing is more accountable than traditional marketing, its focus is to drive results, whereas traditional marketing's focus is on initiating customer interaction. The essence of next-generation marketing is to recognize the shifting roles of traditional and digital marketing in building customer engagement and advocacy. In other words, create symbiosis!

With the internet, you don't need to buy a product to advocate for it. For instance, someone who can't afford to buy a Tesla but is a car enthusiast can still express their admiration for it. There are 3 kinds of media today: paid, owned, and earned media (all thanks to the internet). Earned media is considered the most important today, especially among small & media sized businesses. Why? Because it's free and believable. According to Lindsay Kolowich Cox, earned media, or earned content, is any material written about a business that they haven't paid for or created themselves.

Although this type of media is always published by a third party, there are ways marketers can position themselves for earned media opportunities.

---

2 What is Brand Advocacy and who are these Brand Advocates? Brand advocacy excites both inside and outside the organization about a product or service. Brand advocates can be employees, customers, or influencers. They spread the word about a brand much faster than paid advertising would.

When people don't believe advertising anymore, earned media has that credibility that can make or break a product. This explains why there is a focus on organic marketing – a desire to reach an audience through a beautifully designed company website, as well as highly curated social media. Social proof can make or break a brand on social media today.

As users, we can and must learn what social media reveals about media consumption and use this knowledge to break through the post-factual muck, whilst remaining committed to social justice. If the destruction of the "natural order" can also be made entertaining, effective, and even hedonic, then all media makers – from musicians to journalists to university academics publishing research – can claim the idea of "social media". They can do this by producing media and culture that use these hallmarks to undermine the artificial, cruel stability of capitalism, and build something better. If there is a role for media to play in an increasingly unstable world, not just in a journalistic sense but in the broadest sense of the word "media," it can and should be the radical questioning of social media's semblance of inevitability and normalization. In doing so, we can also claim that which doesn't feature in the timeline at all, our future. And for people in charge, the starting point should be antitrust law to restrain – and ideally restructure – the major internet platforms. Left unchecked, the internet platforms will do what they do. The unintended side effects of their success will continue to harm more than three billion users every day and undermine societies around the world. Ideally, Facebook should become the change agent for protecting its constituents.

Every day, billions of people use Unilever products to feel good, look good and get more out of life. With more than 400 brands bought in 190 countries, they work with consumers to make sustainable living commonplace. Unilever started out in Victorian England in the 1890s with the mission to make cleanliness the new normal; to lessen work for women; to foster health and contribute to personal attractiveness; to make life more enjoyable and rewarding for the people who use their products. Their logo was designed to include 25 icons, each of which represents something important to Unilever. From a lock of hair symbolizing their shampoo brands to a spoon, an ice cream, a jar, a tea leaf, a hand and much more – the little icons all have a meaning. Unilever is a transnational consumer goods company, but to anyone who uses their products around the world, it feels like a homegrown brand. Their core values like integrity, responsibility, respect, and pioneering are what guide their people in the decisions and actions they take every day. Unilever use advertising and marketing to engage with consumers on issues that matter to them.

For a moment, let's also talk about the huge benefits of advertising. Through advertising, brands can communicate their latest innovations, inform consumers about what's in their products and recommend how they should be used. They can even help us change society for the better: Dove's Campaign for Real Beauty challenged stereotypes about the way people look. In general, Dove do not target children under six years or use size zero models in their advertising. So yes, advertising can have a positive impact.

There is much debate around the fashion and marketing industries' portrayal of unrealistic standards of beauty. Unilever brands are free to choose the type of model and actor that best fits the image of the brand. However, they are always bound by Unilever's standards on healthy body image. Fair & Lovely is a skin-lightening cream, infamous for being the best in the world. Its brand essence of 'Rescripting Destiny" has played a decisive role in over 30 countries, where it has been identified as a trusted and super brand. Unilever patented the brand Fair & Lovely in 1971 after the patenting of niacinamide – a melanin suppressor, which is the cream's main active ingredient. In human skin, melanogenesis is initiated by exposure to UV radiation, causing skin to darken. Based on this, Fair & Lovely is a great product for skin flushing, acne treatment and protection from UVB radiation damage. Yet its advertising campaigns communicate fairness, sometimes many shades lighter. For a company like Unilever who takes pride in advertising campaigns that promote real beauty, brand messages like "rescripting destiny" sends the wrong message. In India, where fair is considered beautiful[3], promoting man shades lighter will drive revenue, but it is also enabling systemic issues like colourism, patriarchy, and residual colonialism. They need to instead drive awareness about the harmful effects of UVB radiation on our skin and promote real beauty – irrespective of race, colour, and size. Not re-scripting one's destiny by becoming a few shades lighter. That is considered the insertion of a commercial logic of "fair is beautiful" into aspects of culture that simply aren't true and go against Unilever's core values. Perhaps Unilever's Dove "Real

3 The country's fixation with light skin is a brazen cocktail of colourism, patriarchy, and residual co- lonialism. Fair skin has long been part of India's national psyche. The various settlers, rulers, invaders, and colonizers who entered India starting in the 1400s were relatively light skinned. This includes the Dutch, French, Portuguese, Mughals, and of course, the British, who were in India from the 17th century until India's independence in 1947. During the British Empire, skin tone prejudice became formally en- grained; the colonizers kept light skinned Indians as allies, giving them extra advantages over the rest of the "blacks." The British East India Company even named their settlement at Fort St. George "White Town" and their Indian settlement "Black Town." In June 2017, research firm Global Industry Analysts released a report projecting that global spending on skin lightening will triple to $31.2 billion by 2024. India and China have the highest estimated growth rate. The driving force, the report says, is "the still-rampant darker skin stigma, and a rigid cultural perception that correlates lighter skin tone with beauty and personal success." (Dixit, 2021)

Beauty" Campaign is a conscious evolution from years of advertising that focused on "Rescripting Destiny"?

The Evolution of the Advertising Industry

When Google introduced the cost-per-click advertising buying model, the industry evolved from cost-per-impression to a buying model where advertisers paid only if the audience engaged with the advertisement by clicking on it. As users, we all love YouTube's skip button – but what this button means is that if you don't watch more than six seconds; advertisers don't have to pay. As an advertiser, they don't pay unless somebody watches over 6 seconds of their ad. Now take a brand like McDonald's – they have the resources to do a really good job at creating the ultimate six-second ad, and thereby essentially communicating their slogan for free.

So where are we today?

Advertisers are experiencing advertising avoidance. They are implementing non-traditional plans to tackle this problem. Social Media has enhanced the earned media environment, and as advertisers its more important than ever before to connect with the audience on a personal and emotional level. FMCG brands like Unilever understand that consumers today prefer sustainable brands – and sustainability is all about creating value for all.

Users who tend to avoid advertisements prefer the subscription model. And this business model with its recurring, predictable revenue, belongs to high-performing, superstar media. Simply put, if advertisers and platforms are not collecting your data, it means you're paying them not to – through subscription models.

Marketing and advertising aren't dead, nor are they dying. It is simply evolving. As long as there are products to sell or to be consumed, marketing and advertising will exist. The future is in restructuring our style of management – not just marketing and advertising campaigns.

The Future of Management is Teal Management

Human beings are social species, wired to connect. Connections make us feel heard and understood and give us a sense of belonging. At work, we long for soulful workplaces, for authenticity, community, passion sometimes compassion, and purpose. Turning these dreams into reality lies with enlightened management. The trouble is, when individuals go through an inner transformation, more often than not, they leave the company. This happened to me in 2016. A series of events led to an inner evolution that no longer aligned with the organizational structures and practices that I was a part of. Considering my experience and maturity at that time, it was the doom and gloom of marketing & management activities that enabled this existential action. I decided to go back to school to unlearn my judgements about the industry while learning how to do the same things in different ways.

According to Frederic Laloux, a former McKinsey & Company executive, every time humanity shifted to a new stage of consciousness, it invented a whole new way to structure and run organizations – each time bringing extraordinary breakthroughs in collaboration. A new shift in consciousness is currently underway.

In 2014, Frederic Laloux, after years of searching for a more efficient organizational model, created Teal Organizations. The main objective of this organizational theory is to leverage the complementary talents of employees, by pooling their knowledge and integrating at all levels. The Teal organization is about creating a mature architecture that helps the "humane" element thrive. People transitioning to Teal experience an evolution in consciousness, a momentum driving them towards ever more complex and refined ways of dealing with the world. Each shift occurs when we are able to reach a higher vantage point, from which we see the world in a broader perspective.

There's an extraordinary transformation in consciousness currently taking place worldwide. I asked myself, could we invent a more powerful, more soulful, more meaningful way to work together by changing our belief system? I asked myself this question based on my decade long experience in this industry, and I couldn't think of how this beautiful theory would translate into everyday practicality? Perhaps that is the beauty of evolutionary purpose, we are constantly asking ourselves are we serving the greater good that matters?

DV Media Co. is an extension of my consciousness and my passion for marketing. Even though I went through a shift in my consciousness my love and curiosity about my industry didn't change. I was not ready to break up with marketing. Going back to school during a crisis helped me unlearn and get some guidance on what steps I needed to take to develop my relationship with marketing and set healthy boundaries while doing so. Marketing isn't going away and as marketers our solution isn't to leave the agencies we work for. We must change and in the process of changing existing culture we shall innovate. In Built to Last, (Collins & Porras, 2002) takes readers through Continuity and Change in Visionary Companies; Preserve: core values and core purpose and Change: Culture & operating practices and specific goals and strategies. When I decided to execute my ambition of doing the same thing in a different way, my primary focus was to set up a Teal Agency, just like Frederic Laloux's breakthrough. To give you a better idea of Teal here are the colours that come before Teal:

- **Red Organizations**: A constant exercise of power by chief to keep foot soldiers in line. They are highly reactive and short-term focused. This style thrives in chaotic environments.
- **Amber Organizations**: Highly formal roles within a hierarchical pyramid. They have top-down command and control. In this style the future is repetition of the past.
- **Orange Organizations**: The goal is to beat the competition and achieve high profit and growth. This style incorporates management by objectives.
- **Green Organizations**: A focus on culture and empowerment to boost employee motivation.
- **Teal Organizations**: Self-management replaces hierarchical pyramids. Organizations are seen as living entities, oriented toward realizing their potential.

At DV Media Co. the purpose is to build, nurture and implement purpose-driven movements. The digital playground is vast, accessible, and lush with opportunities. By using it mindfully and creatively, we tap into its potential to create positive change. We believe the most effective way to bring value to brands is to become their partner. This gives us the opportunity to manifest success, and enable meaningful, enduring impact. We are encouraging to stop operating in SILOS – after all, they are separated from one another. When the industry separated media and creative, client value went downhill. To create maximum value, we need to operate from a place of unity.

By contrast to Teal, Red Organization's glue is the continuous exercise of power in interpersonal relationships. The advent of Amber organizations brought about two major breakthroughs: organizations can now plan for the medium and long term, and they can create organizational structures that are stable and scalable. Amber Organizations bring stability to power, with formal titles, fixed hierarchies, and organization charts. The overall structure settles into a rigid pyramid, with a cascade of formal reporting lines from bosses to subordinates.

When pondering about the future of my work and industry, I asked myself the following:

- If for a moment you try to take yourself (your wishes, your dreams) out of the equation and listen to the budding organization, what is the purpose it wants to serve?
- What shape does the organization want to take?
- At what pace does the organization want to grow?
- Is the organization best served by you being a single founder or by several co-founders? Which other co-founders are meant to join you?

The presence and consciousness that I bring as a founder will affect the level of consciousness at which the organization operates.

Teal Organizations have found the key to operating effectively, even at a large scale – with a system based on peer relationships, without the need for either hierarchy or consensus. Teal Management is the decentralization of management styles.

Organizations have always been places that encourage people to show up with a narrow "professional" self and to check other parts of the self at the door. They often require us to show a masculine resolve, to display determination and strength, and to hide doubts and vulnerability. Rationality is king, while the emotional, intuitive, spiritual parts of ourselves often feel unwelcome – out of place. Teal Organizations have developed a consistent set of practices that invite us to reclaim our inner wholeness and bring our complete and entire selves to work.

Teal Organizations are seen as having a life and a sense of direction of their own. Instead of trying to predict and control the future, members of the organization are invited to listen in and understand what the organization wants to become; what purpose it wants to serve. This is exactly what we need today!

We know corporate governance practices have tightly linked the purpose of business with maximizing shareholder value. However, as the 21st century pushes on, there's been an increased emphasis on other stakeholder values, particularly social and environmental concerns. This trend in corporate governance – which has led to the growth in "triple-bottom line" thinking – has fuelled the emergence of a new organizational form: the Certified B Corporation in United States of America. B Corporations demonstrate that a firm is following a fundamentally different governance philosophy than a traditional shareholder-centred corporation. Identifying as a B corporation is a way to publicly claim an identity as an organization interested in both shareholder and stakeholder success. Having a clear identity can help firms communicate their values to customers, which is particularly beneficial when they are claiming an identity different from the industry norm. An unconventional identity – such as a B Corporation – helps individuals clearly distinguish between traditional firms and those that are committed to a broader set of stakeholder values.

For mission-driven businesses, these alternative forms of organizing provide an opportunity to better communicate their commitment to society and to the natural environment in a world where everybody claims to be "green" and "good." While B corp may not be a global phenomenon yet, perhaps this is something law makers could think about adopting.

We exist in an age where technology has shifted the paradigm for human cognition and interaction entirely. We've reached a nexus in time where digital skills are no longer considerations or afterthoughts, but imperative if we want our species to coexist against increasingly complex technologies and systems.

Being part of the digital landscape means we're no strangers to the problematic issues around selective censorship, polarization, misinformation, abuse of personalized data and addiction. In that light, digital literacy and responsibility is the need of the hour. Brands, companies, and organizations need to lay the foundations for a relationship with the digital marketing space – now more than ever. We are at the genesis of a new age, we must open ourselves to the idea of radical transparency and agility. Because radical transparency builds trust and being truly agile connects everyone and everything, all the time. It has the capability to deliver intimate, instant, frictionless value at scale.

Within my own borders, India's digital penetration has crossed 700 million people and is rising exponentially. The country's technological evolution has turned digital media forms such as social networking apps into a source of news, opinion, social interaction, and subsequent validation.

For any business, digital media, specifically social media, is a double-edged sword. It can become a company's most dynamic friend if used to express why it does what it does, how it's done and what value it brings you. Contrastingly, it can also become an organization's worst enemy if used irresponsibly, or to manipulate the general population and spread misinformation.

The role of a digital agency then becomes all the more crucial, given the current state of affairs. This power comes with responsibility – which poses the question of whether the voice we create will be honest and authentic or fake and manipulative.

A digital agency operates in an always "ON" business environment, where one click could make or break a brand's voice. An agency's role is multifold, from sifting through all kinds of content, to mindfully and strategically, placing it. An agency has to position its clients in a safe space on this ever-expanding spectrum. Where they can reside as social beings with a digital presence – the most important presence today.

So how does a digital agency develop its own approach to presenting its clients and itself?

What is it that people value in a space saturated with information and opinions?

Something that has previously lurked in the darkness but has come to prominence today as a one-step solution to poignancy and market penetration – transparency. Positively conceived by society as a sign of 'clean' and 'pure'. This form of being is associated with unequivocal honesty and provides an unfiltered view of the shape of things.

What if we incorporate transparency as a value system? The concept of transparency is, of course, complex and multidimensional. I decided to look within our own team to find answers about how to move the needle towards the sustainable future we envision for ourselves through digital media transformation. For organizations, transparency is an instant selling mix that drives people to buy your products, consume your media and use your services. In campaigns, this element of transparency acts as a voice of authority. When an organization tries to create demand by addressing a need or finding a problem and presenting the solution, the truth becomes the most valuable element in its pitch. People are waiting to be 'moved'.

For Indians, we are rethinking 'our social customs'. Several marketing agencies have been successful primarily because they give us practices and beliefs that require questioning, reach the masses through careful placement and oftentimes change the way people view their client's products or services.

It's important to acknowledge that transparency manifests itself with context. Among team members at a digital agency, it helps with setting clear milestones and targets, as well as with managing expectations. When all team members know clearly where a project is headed and how management wants to execute a project, a team member can manage their time better, set coherent targets and calibrate the effort they invest.

Transparency within an agency stems from inclusivity, which can be an uplifting experience for everyone who works there. It helps build a stronger team for the future and instils trust within all team members, knowing they are included and are up to date with developments – be it with clients or within the organization. Transparency promotes highlighting the different thought processes prevalent within a workforce, training us to be more accepting of opinions we may not agree with, but must respect, encouraging inclusivity.

It is however important to be transparent with their brand partner from the perspective of setting expectations and benchmarking how much the agency can be pushed outside of the defined scope of work, which is (obviously) crucial for a healthy and long-lasting collaboration. On the flip side, an agency, as the executor of a brand's image, is dependent on the organization's transparency. The organization's willingness to share information regarding their products/services/mission is essential to fluid workflow.

Transparency is a key cog in an organization's self-awareness – when an organization can look within, acknowledge its faults and flaws and use its platform for self-improvement or the improvement the world today. This is where their products come in – either to satisfy that need or simply as a beneficiary to an 'authentic', real campaign. This is a watershed moment for purpose-driven organizations, who must work towards to adopting a more conscious approach at scale.

What if we had the freedom to work independently along with the solidarity of a collective? Jana Murad and Paulina Kay, the founders of Good Intentions Creative Studio in London, share, "The ability to understand what kind of environments are conducive for maximum creativity is key. As such, being self-aware and in tune with your own intuition is the answer."

Allyship is an important part of this approach – instead of seeing another digital agency as competition, we must view them as allies, whose values align with ours. This is something visionary companies do; they are in competition with themselves to do better. Imagine working on a project with varied voices and collaborate across borders. Some of the benefits of working in a collaborative environment are that we can include a plurality of perspectives, identify errors faster and, ultimately, find unique solutions to problems.

With globalization at our fingertips or in a glocal[4] economy, we must use collaboration as a tool to bring beneficial perspectives and a systems-approach to generating ideas, collaborative working value possibilities, stability, challenges and connections.

So many components of our existence are being radically reconfigured and updated right now. Why should it be any different when it comes to our work environment?

Let's build a community of media experts who build projects in tandem – all about team-focused working. Collaboration helps identify the right people for a specific project; so that we can put together the perfect team for each assignment we take on. Additionally set up a collaborative environment that is non-hierarchical; the team may have a leader, but they're more like a guardian or driver of the project who makes sure the team is on track.

I believe that collaborative networks represent a promising paradigm in a knowledge-driven society and can equip us to better deal with the rapidly evolving challenges we are faced with today as business entities, and as a society in general. Change, investigation, mindfulness and purpose are at the crux of every aspect of a good process and business.

Purpose grew out of a post-2008 belief that business needs to redefine its role and relationship with society, and that companies can be a force for good. Instead of limiting their focus on generating value for shareholders, businesses can adopt the idea of creating shared value for all.

For instance – Mandalah is an organization that I really admire; they describe themselves as conscious innovation partners. One global team made up of people from all walks of life who collectively value plurality as a means to amplify the unique lenses through which they take on their projects.

---

4 Describing the seamless integration between the local and global; the comprehensive con- nect-edness produced by travel, business, and communications; willingness and ability to think globally and act locally. 'The concept of glocalization captures the dynamic, contingent, and two-way dialectic between the global and the local' (Swyngedouw (2004) Camb. Rev. Int. Affairs 17).

"Each individual has unique gifts, talents and skills," says John J. Murphy, a specialist in business transformation and author of Pulling Together: 10 Rules for High-Performance Teamwork. "When we bring them to the table and share them for a common purpose, it can give companies a real advantage."

Digital media is an evolving organism that constantly challenges brands and consumers alike to stay on top of things. We make sure we are updated on the most cutting-edge ways to build businesses online and working together in an ever-changing environment ensures that we view our work through an evolutionary lens.

Working together in collaborative networks triggers teamwork, debate and a sense of agility. Creativity and collaboration know no bounds — something I witnessed first-hand for time while working on a project in New York.

With transparency and collaboration inclusivity and diversity comes naturally. The concept of diversity is, of course, complex and multidimensional, to find answers about how to move the needle towards the sustainable future we envision for ourselves through the lens of digital media transformation.

I watched a documentary on one of the world's most admired conservationists, Jane Goodall, and her work on chimpanzee research. I was transfixed, absolutely amazed, as a chimpanzee used a twig as a fishing rod to extract termites from the mounds before gobbling them up.

This brought me back to the idea that absolutely anybody – even a chimpanzee! – can be creative, given the right opportunities and resources.

For media folks looking to make a mark in the digital media space – here's your chance to do the same thing in a different way. Work to reside at the intersection of creative and analytical, tempered with a dose of self-management, a sense of wholeness and evolutionary purpose.

The Turkish-British storyteller and novelist Elif Shafak hits the nail on the head in her 2017 TED talk when she explains that singularity is an illusion – because we all have a multiplicity of voices inside us. The Persian poet Hafiz used to say, "You carry in your soul every ingredient necessary to turn your existence into joy. All you have to do is mix those ingredients."

I believe that the essence of the human psyche is the same across cultures. So, a pool of talented experts whose specialties span a whole diversity of skills is a fitting formula for this petri dish experiment.

Why is this important? So that we can learn – as a professional community – to accept differences; to be tolerant towards something we may not completely understand at first. We must yearn to see the beauty and strength in a variety of people, communities and ideas.

By including and acknowledging the co-existence of different thought processes and specializations, we are paving the path to building a sustainable co-working ecosystem.

I am guided by making diversity a business priority. How else could we create true opportunities for all, regardless of the variables? It's about changing mindsets as a stepping stone in creating the kind of future we want to live and work in. The data for diversity and innovation speaks for itself.

What does the next generation of marketing look like?

Holistic media solutions are the way forward – we can no longer look at any story or idea in isolation. We must instead examine how it is inter-connected within the larger conversation of storytelling and digital marketing. And we know all too well by now just how much more conversations we need to be having immediately in order to create a sustainable future.

Diversity – of thoughts, ideas and interests – has an uncanny way of promoting out-of-the-box thinking. And we're all about out-of-the-box ideas and getting out of our comfort zones.

Think about it – Steve Jobs came up with the idea to start Apple not when he was studying computer engineering, but when he took a semester in calligraphy!

Cultivating domain expertise, encouraging experimentation with adjacent interests and empowering oneself with technical know-how – these three steps will set you right on the path to diverse ideation.

We have more things in common today – across borders and cultures – than we don't. It's time to leverage this. To tell any story accurately, we need to investigate all its different angles for a well-rounded outlook. If we focus on a single story, we risk a critical misunderstanding. In this new era, partner with clients and collaborators of varied backgrounds to encourage mutual growth so that we all rise in tandem.

With experts of various specializations looking at the same proposals from different points of view, we study all opportunities holistically. Once an idea is approached holistically, innovation is the next natural step.

What's revolutionary about creative thinking is that one word or reference can spark a ground-breaking idea in a whole other sphere. Designers can now collaborate across borders, business owners can access the work of specialists in different fields with a quick glance through their websites – the present-day business card, if you will.

Put simply – it's walking the talk of our values. The equal representation of thoughts, ideas, cultures and people – regardless of gender, nationality, age, industry, career and education.

It also means working with specialists across borders and cultures, while retaining autonomy in our own domain. In Built to Last, (Collins & Porras, 2002) breaks down a few myths around the formula we pitched here (Purpose + Values = Vision) and this particular one made me pause and reflect on how Teal Management, operating from core purpose and values would look like in the future:

Myth: Visionary companies are great places to work, for everyone.

Reality: Only those who "fit" extremely well with the core ideology and demanding standard of a visionary company will find it a great place to work.

If you go to work at a visionary company, you will either fit & flourish – probably couldn't be happier – or you will likely be expunged like a virus. Its binary. There is no middle ground. It's almost cult-like. Visionary companies are so clear about what they stand for and what they're trying to achieve that they simply don't have room for those unwilling or unable to fit their exacting standards.

Radical Transparency, Collaboration, Integrity, and Diversity give access to opportunities that suit a skill set based on merit, past experience and willingness to grow and evolve with the constantly changing demands of the fast-paced digital environment. It also means working with specialists across borders and cultures, while retaining autonomy in our own domain. As we enter a new era, let's embrace this glorious melting pot.

Epilogue: Is this the End, Beautiful Friend?
Amina Qureshi & Dona Varghese

"...most men and women will grow up to love their servitude and will never dream of revolution."
- Brave New World

This chapter may feel heavier or more personal – because it is. It's a reflection of the "so what?" that we're all left asking ourselves at the end of it all. Why does it all matter? There are several ways to slice and dice this, but for me, it's always been about asking whether we are leaving the world in a better state than we found it. In the end, can we comfortably say we did everything within our power – whatever that may be – to create a more just, more compassionate, more connected world?

I was never a righteous person, so my battle against Facebook never seemed to stem from a moralistic belief in right vs. wrong. I told myself that it stemmed from the fact that I was working in an industry with players like Facebook – wielding greater power than they deserved, abusing that power, and continuing to permeate every aspect of our lives without a second thought of consideration to its intended or unintended effects. But the real reason it mattered to me? In the end, it mattered because in 2017, my son was born. And obviously, he changed my life.

You always hear parents say that. That having kids has morphed them into better people. I don't know if that's true, but I do know that children make you think about the world differently. Understanding the world through the lens of a child enabled me to think critically again. About what kind of structures we're putting in place societally to better ourselves. And Facebook never seems to line up. It began as this beautiful promise to bring an increasingly isolated and lonely world back together through community-building. But somewhere along the way, connecting communities devolved into just another marketing tagline. Whether Zuckerberg set out to amass unprecedented power, or whether he continues to intentionally prioritize profits over the commonwealth of our society – remains to be seen.

In the end, everyone is going to have a different point of view about the good, the bad and the ugly sides of Facebook. What we leave you with, is merely a point of view from two industry insiders. Two South Asian women working in advertising for several decades; the work spanning the globe from India to Dubai to Toronto. Our beliefs are, of course, rooted in fundamental facts about Facebook and its various indiscretions pertaining to data, privacy and monopolistic practices. But the real reason why Facebook must be stopped was always a personal one.

From a parent's perspective, the thought of having my son entrenched in a meta world devoid of physical relationships gives me a visceral reaction of sadness. I truly can't imagine a more disengaged existence. The best-case scenario is a future where we blend digital with analog by giving ourselves the time that we need to disconnect. Slow down, and appreciate the real and fundamental relationships in our lives rather than the avatar versions of our relationships.

I want my son to grow up feeling freedom. Knowing what it feels like to have butterflies in his stomach from meeting that special someone who blows him away. I want him to feel what it's like to enjoy late-night evenings having home-cooked food with friends over too many bottles of wine. I want him to know what it feels like to have his own family one day and be absolutely immersed in their lives without the constant distraction of screens. These experiences cannot be replicated in any future version of a meta world.

Scott Galloway often says that a mother's irrational passion for her child's success is the greatest predictor of that child's happiness. If that's true, and I believe that it is, it requires maddening amounts of time, devotion, patience and engagement. It requires that child to go out in the world and try things – untethered by social media and its addictive lure. It requires a parent to be present and attentive – two characteristics that are often disregarded when we're constantly living behind a screen.

Developing relationships is hard work, but it always pays off. It requires giving a shit about people. And nothing implicitly translates to "I don't care about what you're saying" more than being on your phone while someone is speaking to you. Why are we more willing to give our time and attention to strangers on the Internet, scrolling endlessly through our feeds, rather than to our parents, our peers, our co-workers and our children?

I believe the answer lies in the inability to stop and think – actually think – about the impact of being so fully, so wholly absorbed in social media. This book is mostly about Facebook, because we believe they've transgressed further than any other company. But too much time spent on any one platform is bound to yield similar negative effects. Apple has intentionally built in functionality to address this by providing an option to silence notifications by enabling Focus Time or Sleep Time. In short, the human brain was never designed to deal with so much distraction. We need to unplug.

I was listening to a Sam Harris podcast, in which he posed an interesting question that prompted me to consider whether people should care if they don't have children. In short, why do people care about what happens to the world after they're gone? Particularly if you don't have kids. And particularly if you don't believe in any form of afterlife. Why do we care what happens after we move on? 150 years of study in neurology has shown us that if we damage certain areas of the brain, then certain faculties are lost: recognition, memory, speech – the list goes on. So why then, do we believe that when we die – which in essence, is the destruction of the mind in its entirety – we will still have consciousness or cognition, which we've loosely labelled as our 'spirit'? I don't purport to have answers, but I do know that there's something drastically unsettling about leaving our planet obliterated and uncared for.

"The metaverse is the next frontier in connecting people, just like social networking was when we got started," Zuckerberg shared in a recent founder's letter. "Over time, I hope we are seen as a metaverse company, and I want to anchor our work and our identity on what we're building toward."

The problem, of course, is that Facebook is Meta, and Meta is Facebook. The same issues that plague the social media giant will likely transfer to the potential metaverse giant: the virtual hornet's nest of privacy and tracking questions, the poor relationship with Apple, and the bad reputation Facebook has built over the years.

In the end, no matter how hard I tried to justify more rational reasons for caring, it always boiled down to answering a very simple question: are the actions that we are taking today going to better the world that our children will inherit? Because if the answer is no, and we can acknowledge that the answer is no, then we must take action and pivot. Whether that's through deactivating our Facebook and Instagram accounts as consumers, taking an organizational stance against investing advertising dollars on the platform as a business, or educating our peers and community about the nefarious mechanisms under which Facebook continues to operate.

In our day and age, our attention is incredibly valuable. It is one of the most sacred, most finite resources – and we must do everything to preserve it. Before acknowledging the extent to which our attention is consistently hijacked, I wondered why I always felt drained and out of energy by the end of the day. When my son talked to me, I was constantly distracted. I was more interested in how many 'likes' my most recent photo on Instagram got, than in what one of the most important people in my life had to say.

After leaving Instagram, I felt a renewed sense of time. And after a while, I noticed a perceptible shift in my mental health and overall happiness. There's no specific point in time where I remember a sudden shift, but over time, I stopped comparing my life to others' via Instagram photos. I wasn't draining hours scrolling through, endlessly indulging in other people's lives. I was finally living my own.

When my friend recently asked me why I always seemed grounded and happy, the reason became beyond apparent to me. The compliment paid to me by my friend was amazing, but more importantly, it made me think of the reasons behind this change in myself. Some are obvious – the well-known benefits of exercise and stretching, finding meaning in one's work, developing authentic relationships, eating healthy (I could probably do better here), and limiting drinking wine (I could probably also do better here). But realistically, beyond those changes, the true reason for my happiness was that I was no longer tethered to social media.

On cutting out my socials, it's as if a cord had been cut. It opened a tremendous amount of time for me to begin investing in things, both big and small, that gave me happiness. It just so happened that those things were more often than not – relationships. I had my son, learned to navigate the ins-and-outs of motherhood and I've received the privilege of being present and watching him grow as a 4-year old. When I think about his future, I want it to be invested in relationships with that same level of intensity. I'm not sure how possible this will be in a fully digitized metaverse.

In the end, I am filled with gratitude for working in such a fascinating industry. The tech and advertising industries are total giants in today's world. Tech CEOs have become God-like. And Facebook has dominated and permeated so many aspects of our everyday lives, our society, and our wellbeing. Letting Facebook remain untamed is a misdoing to the shared health of our communities. What started out as a utopia-like promise has since morphed into a dangerous, many-tentacled beast, impacting a whole variety of facets – data, privacy, consumer trust, teen wellbeing, and mental health, just to name a few.

The only prayer I'm left with, is that the unexplored metaverse that we're about to enter is a kind and beautiful one. That we take the very best ideals of humanity and apply them with rigor and respect to the dawn of a new age.

— *Amina Qureshi*

What this book has hopefully illustrated is a pattern of human behaviour in a Brave New Meta World. We set out to write this book in the hopes of revealing the important connections that help explain and critique contemporary technologies and their impact on the way we live and work. The aim is not to leave you completely dangling, but to encourage you to think about the simultaneous realities of the world we live in. When Amina Qureshi and I decided to write this book, we were anxious about the harsh nature of our industry, and terrified knowing we weren't even mid-way through our careers in media and advertising. Rather than instinctively jumping in to solve a problem in heroic leader mode, we instead asked, "what process should we use to solve this problem?" We went back in time to backcast the emergence of the communication industry, in order to forecast the future of it. That was the only way to go about writing this piece.

In his book Media and Modernity (2013), Thompson J. B. encouraged readers to think about the reinvention of publicness. Renumerate on your privacy status to reinvent publicness. In Attention Merchants (2016), Tim Wu proposed the Human Reclamation Project. He compared it to efforts incorporated to reclaim natural resources through conservation and protection. He stated that over the coming century, the most vital human resource in need of conservation and protection is likely to be our own consciousness and mental space. How do we conceptualize this assignment, and what does it look like practically?

To Consumers: reclaim your time and space. Protect your mind palace and interpersonal interactions – in the office, online, your home – any place where we mean to interact with one another or achieve something that requires a serious level of concentration. The best way to live life more meaningfully is to live in one reality at a time. Living life in a state of deep focus and high concentration without distractions will enable a more meaningful, fulfilled life. In the emerging age of godlike technology, we must focus on human beings creating delight for other human beings.

When societies, organizations and politics are populated by people who embrace this mindset, they can be at one with themselves, at one with those for whom the work is being done, at one with those who are doing the work, and at one with the wider society in which it operates. While such a simple goal may claim high praises, it can prove to be surprisingly difficult. What is simple is rarely ever easy. How often have you caught yourself shaming your productivity levels? May it be in the form of checking email, social media apps, random news stories, browsing through OTT platforms, titillating clickbait or simply being a couch potato. Stating that we are busy is the new sexy and the desire to do nothing leads to productivity shame. I am not taking away the fact that many of our most important technologies have enhanced our lives and are serving and advancing humanity like never before. I am simply asking you to choose platforms that aren't designed to faithfully serve their owner's real interests and entirely eat up your time and space. The movement has begun, comprised of individuals who are more careful about how they spend their attention. Consumers, I encourage you to draw the line and reclaim ownership of the very experience of living.

To those working in advertising agencies: I would like to reiterate the famous John Wanamaker quote: "Half the money I spend on advertising is wasted; the trouble is, I don't know which half." We must stop trying to over-justify accountability and measurability to everything that we launch, try opting for radical transparency and improvising. Start with a focus on unified connectivity. Earned media is the most important today because it's free and believable – people don't believe advertising anymore. Earned media has that credibility that can make or break a product. We know marketing isn't going anywhere. As long as ideas exist – marketing will live alongside them. What is changing, is the future of the environment in which these ideas are planted, nurtured, implemented and optimized. Frederic Laloux's Teal Organizations have found the key to operate effectively, even at a large scale, with a system based on peer relationships, without the need for either hierarchy or consensus. Teal Organizations have developed a consistent set of practices that invite us to reclaim our inner wholeness and bring all of "who we are" to work. Instead of trying to predict and control the future, listen in, and understand what the organization wants to become; what purpose it wants to serve, what are its core values. Most importantly let's start admitting that the outcome of marketing is beyond logic. Operate through transparency, collaboration, diversity and from a place of integrity. Fellow colleagues, it's time to draw the line at the over-justification of our performance.

To Brands: it's your dollars. You hold the power. You are the solution. In a world dominated by social media, influencers and earned media, incorporate reach and frequency models that meet at the intersection of purpose and profit. Empower people. Do not destroy them. Focus on capitalism that cares. What steps are you going to take to stimulate a kind of public engagement which is neither centralized nor wholly decentralized? Tim Wu rightly concludes in Attention Merchants: today we see advertising screens in places that are unavoidable, unrequested, and unwelcome, such as waiting rooms or napkins. These instances of "attention theft" take value without compensation. Stop enabling an environment where your consumers are someone else's commodity. You have the power to draw the line between the private and the commercial. Dear Brands, continue to have the eternal debate over whether advertising is good, bad or a necessary evil. Choose where you want to draw the line.

To Big Tech: Yale professor Timothy D. Snyder in his book "The Road to Unfreedom" makes a convincing case that the world is sleepwalking into an Authoritarian Age. You did not cause the current transformation of the world, but you have enabled it, sped it up, and ensured it reaches every corner of the world simultaneously. Your design choices have undermined democracy and civil rights. The war of information was started by you. Our consumption habits are deeply influenced by your algorithms and coded biases. You have the power to be the change we want to see in this world. You could not have imagined the damage to democracy, public health, privacy and competition you enabled instead. For the people living in the United States, United Kingdom or Brazil, their country's politics have been transformed in ways that may persist for generations. For the people in Myanmar or Sri Lanka, their life may have been threatened. In every country with internet access, you have transformed society for the worse. In Tim Wu's convincing observation – you are running an uncontrolled evolutionary experiment, and the results, so far, are terrifying. Tens of millions of people are already effectively citizens of Apple, citizens of Uber, citizens of Amazon, citizens of your platforms. You have carefully cultivated supply and demand for two things people are desperately seeking: validation and hope. Tech tycoons profit on such palaeolithic human tendencies. In fact, it seems they are not interested in drawing a line at all. Please prove us wrong.

To Journalists: all media makers, from bloggers to journalists to university academics publishing research – don't you want to build something better? It's your time to reclaim the idea of social media, by producing media and culture that use hallmarks to undermine the artificial, cruel and unstable current scenario. If there is a role for journalists to play in an increasingly unstable world, it can and should be the normalization of radical questioning on the War of Information. Draw the line and claim that which doesn't feature in the timeline at all: The Future.

To Governments: your starting point is applying antitrust law to restrain, and ideally restructure, the major internet platforms. Left unchecked, the internet platforms will do what they do. In this book, we outlined the possible steps to take in using online media more responsibly, whether for the dissemination of information or for other purposes. In any case, the solution to colossally complex problems is rarely "more control." The answers, if they can be found, will not lie with consumers, brands, tech tycoons or journalists at all, but in the kind of society we have, and the kind of society we want. Governments – it's up to you to draw the line of change – not control.

Over the last seventeen months, we've had countless conversations with experts and colleagues around the world, on every aspect of our story. Learning from them has been the high point of our journey. We anticipate many of you will know about at least some aspects of the story we told. But our hope is that the overall narrative we offered will inspire most of you to look differently at Digitization, Marketing, Data, Communication and Technology.

The argument we put forward is neither easy nor simple; it requires effort to consider how the economy and society work, and to appreciate and work out alternative perspectives.
We encourage you to reflect and think about the Future of Media and Technology. Whoever you are. Whatever you do. Because that's the only way to brave the new world we are headed toward.

— *Dona Varghese*

References

1. #136 - Digital Humanism. (n.d.). Sam Harris. https://samharris. org/ podcasts/making-sense-episodes/136-digital-humanism

2. #218 - Welcome to the Cult Factory. (2020, September 25). Sam Harris. https://samharris.org/podcasts/making-sense- episodes/218-welcome-cult-factory

3. Benner, K., & Ember, S. (2015, September 19). Enabling of Ad Blocking in Apple's iOS 9 Prompts Backlash. The New York Times. https://www.nytimes.com/2015/09/19/technology/apple-ios-9s-enabling-of-ad-blocking-prompts-backlash.html?smid=pl-share

4. Carr, D. (2010, January 1). Why Twitter Will Endure. The New York Times. https://www.nytimes.com/2010/01/03/weekinreview/03carr.html

5. Cass Sunstein | How to Defuse Polarization and Bridge Divides in Business, Politics and Society. (2020, October 29). YouTube. https://www. youtube.com/watch?v=2ay_DJGs_cc

6. The COVID-19 Pandemic Has Led to a Surge of Socially Responsible Behaviors According to Special Release of the Conscious Consumer Spending Index (#CCSIndex). (2020, May 21). Good Must Grow. https://www.csrwire.com/press_releases/45174-the-covid-19-pandemic-has-led-to-a-surge-of-socially-responsible-behaviors- according-to-special-release-of-the-conscious-consumer-spending- index-ccsindex-

7. Deibert, R. J. (1997). Parchment, Printing, and Hypermedia. Columbia Univ Pr.

8. Druckman, J. N. (2020, November 23). Affective polarization, local contexts and public opinion in America. Nature. https://www. nature.com/articles/s41562-020-01012-5?error=cookies_not_ supported&code=b235f461-c319-4976-8e2e-5171c48769d3

9. The Economics of Attention. (2016, November 22). YouTube. https://www.youtube.com/watch?v=5z4RS_5tZIA

10. Gorgone, K. O. (2018, April 18). Doing Well, Doing Good, and Doing Right: Nichole Kelly Explains "Conscious Marketing" on Marketing Smarts [Podcast]. Marketing Profs. https://www.marketingprofs. com/ podcasts/2018/34190/conscious-marketing-nichole-kelly- marketing-smarts

11. Graber, C. (2007, November 1). Snake Oil Salesmen Were on to Something. Scientific American. https://www.scientificamerican. com/ article/snake-oil-salesmen-knew-something/

12. The Great Hack's David Carroll finally sees his Cambridge Analytica data. (2020, September 29). YouTube. https://www.youtube. com/ watch?v=5Swqc2NjEXM

13. Horwitz, J. (2021, January 31). Facebook Knew Calls for Violence Plagued 'Groups,' Now Plans Overhaul. WSJ. https://www.wsj.com/ articles/facebook-knew-calls-for-violence-plagued-groups-now-plans-overhaul-11612131374

14. Journalism That Stands Apart. (2017, January 1). The New York Times Company. https://www.nytimes.com/projects/2020-report/ index.html

15. Laloux, F., & Appert, E. (2016). Reinventing Organizations: An Illustrated Invitation to Join the Conversation on Next-Stage Organizations. Nelson Parker.

16. Lapowsky, I. (2019, January 25). One Man's Obsessive Fight to Reclaim His Cambridge Analytica Data. Wired. https://www.wired. com/story/one-mans-obsessive-fight-to-reclaim-his-cambridge- analytica-data/

17. Maddox, J. (2022, March 10). Ukraine's Twitter account is a national version of real-time trauma processing. The Conversation. https://theconversation.com/ukraines-twitter-account-is-a-national-version-of-real-time-trauma-processing-178278

18. Our ongoing approach to the war in Ukraine. (2022, March 16). Twitter Blog. https://blog.twitter.com/en_us/topics/ company/2022/our-ongoing-approach-to-the-war-in-ukraine

19. Patreon CEO Jack Conte on why creators can't depend on platforms. (2021, June 22). Spotify. https://open.spotify.com episode/71XfOozM9BNrtVTAu41VSN?si= aL3d4Ss5R7C7WSLkKIfKtw

20. Pegoraro, R. U. T. (2016, June 5). Status with Facebook "interest- based" ads is complicated. USA TODAY. https://eu.usatoday.com/ story/tech/columnist/2016/06/05/status-facebook-interest-based-ads-complicated/85448476/

21. Safety on. (2022, February 26). Twitter. https://twitter.com/TwitterSafety/ status/1497353965419257860?ref_src=twsrc%5Etfw%7Ctwcamp%5Etweetembed%7Ctwterm% 5E1497353965419257860%7Ctwgr%5E%7Ctwcon%5

Es1_&ref_url=https%3A%2F%2Fblog.twitter.com%2Fen_us%2Ftopics%2Fcompany%2F

2022%2Four-ongoing-approach-to-the-war-in-ukraine

22. Sam Harris | Can We Avoid a Digital Apocalypse? (n.d.). Sam Harris. https://samharris.org/blog/can-we-avoid-a-digital-apocalypse

23. Why Companies Are Becoming B Corporations. (2017, June 22). Harvard Business Review. https://hbr.org/2016/06/why- companies-are-becoming-b-corporations

24. Thomas De Zengotita. Mediated - How the media shapes your world and the way you live in it. 2005

25. Viktor Mayer-Schonberger & Thomas Ramge. Reinventing Capitalism - in the Age of Big Data. 2018

26.   Tim Wu. The Attention Merchants - The Epic scramble to get inside our heads. 2017

27.   Benedict Anderson. Imagined Communities - Reflections on the Origin and spread of Nationalism. 1983

28.   Julian Assange, et al. Cypherpunks - Freedom and the future of the internet. 2016

29.   Joshua Foa Dienstag. Pessimism - Philosophy, Ethics and Spirit. 2006

30.   Ozlem Sensoy, et al. Is everyone really equal? An introduction to key concepts in social justice education. 2017

31.   Roger McNamee. Zucked - Waking up to the Facebook Catastrophe. 2019

32.   Yuval Noah Harari. 21 Lessons for the 21st Century. 2018

33.   John B. Thompson. The Media and Modernity - A social theory of the Media. 1995

34.   Derek Thompson. Hit Makers - How to succeed in an age of distraction. 2017

35.   Steven Johnson. Where do good ideas come from? 2010

36.   Marcus Gilroy-Ware. Filling the void - emotion, capitalism & social media. 2017

37.   Chip Heath & Dan Heath. Made to Stick - Why some ideas survive, and others die. 2007

38.   Scott Galloway. The Four - The hidden DNA of Amazon, Apple, Facebook & Google. 2017

39.   53 Incredible Facebook Statistics and Facts. (2019, June 1). Brandwatch. https://www.brandwatch.com/blog/facebook-statistics/

40.   Bergman, D. (2022, January 31). Does Being a "Legacy" Increase Your Admission Odds? College Transitions. https://www.collegetransitions.com/blog/college-legacy/

41.   Brandon, J. (2021, January 5). These Updated Stats About How Often You Use Your Phone Will Humble You. Inc.Com. https://www. inc.com/john-brandon/these-updated-stats-about-how-often-we- use-our-phones-will-humble-you.html

42.   Clare Duffy, CNN Business. (2021, October 25). Facebook, Instagram almost banned from App Store in 2019 over human trafficking content. CNN. https://edition.cnn.com/2021/10/25/tech/facebook-instagram-app-store-ban-human-trafficking/index.html

43.   Cox, J. (2019, August 16). CEOs see pay grow 1,000% in the last 40 years, now make 278 times the average worker. CNBC. https:// www.cnbc.com/2019/08/16/ceos-see-pay-grow-1000percent-and- now-make-278-times-the-average-worker.html#:%7E:text=The%20 pay%20gap%20between%20top,278%20times%20the%20 average%20worker.

44. Disconnect between brain's dopamine system and cocaine addiction. (2019, January 10). ScienceDaily. https://www. sciencedaily.com/releases/2019/01/190110141803.htm

45. Facebook froze as anti-vaccine comments swarmed users. (2021, October 26). AP NEWS. https://apnews.com/article/the-facebook- papers-covid-vaccine-misinformation-c8bbc569be7cc2ca583dadb 4236a0613

46. Fiegerman, S. (2022, March 11). This Is What Facebook's First Ads Looked Like. Mashable. https://mashable.com/archive/facebook-first-ad

47. Hagey, K., & Horwitz, J. (2021, September 15). Facebook Tried to Make Its Platform a Healthier Place. It Got Angrier Instead. WSJ. https://www.wsj.com/articles/facebook-algorithm-change- zuckerberg-11631654215?mod=article_inline

48. Hakim, D., & Rosenberg, M. (2018, March 19). Data Firm Tied to Trump Campaign Talked Business With Russians. The New York Times. https://www.nytimes.com/2018/03/17/us/politics/ cambridge-analytica-russia.html

49. Isaac, M. (2021, July 28). Facebook's profit surges 101 percent on strong ad sales. The New York Times. https://www.nytimes. com/2021/07/28/business/facebook-q2-earnings.html

50. Puiu, T. (2021, May 13). Your smartphone is millions of times more powerful than the Apollo 11 guidance computers. ZME Science. https://www.zmescience.com/science/news-science/smartphone- power-compared-to-apollo-432/

51. Satariano, A. (2021, October 7). Facebook Hearing Bolsters Calls for Regulation in Europe. The New York Times. https://www. nytimes.com/2021/10/06/technology/facebook-european-union- regulation.html

52. Savage, C. (2014, June 25). Between the Lines of the Cellphone Privacy Ruling. The New York Times. https:// www.nytimes.com/ interactive/2014/06/25/us/ annotated-supreme-court-cellphoneprivacy-decision. html?mtrref=undefined&gwh=2FB188230ED092059D5 031E477D74CAE&gwt=pay&assetType=PAYWALL

53. Schomer, A. A. D. A. W. (2021, October 25). Digital Trust Benchmark Report 2021. Insider Intelligence. https://www.emarketer. com/ content/digital-trust-benchmark-report-2021

54. Statista. (2022, June 24). Global advertising revenue 2012– 2027. https://www.statista.com/statistics/236943/global-advertising-spending/

55. Wang, A. B. (2017, December 12). Former Facebook VP says social media is destroying society with 'dopamine-driven feedback loops.' Washington Post. https://www.washingtonpost.com/ news/ the-switch/wp/2017/12/12/former-facebook-vp-says- social-media-is-

destroying-society-with-dopamine-driven-feedback- loops/?noredirect=on

56. Weisbaum, H. (2018, April 18). Trust in Facebook has dropped by 66 percent since the Cambridge Analytica scandal. NBC News. https://www.nbcnews.com/business/consumer/trust-facebook- has-dropped-51-percent-cambridge-analytica-scandal-n867011

57. Wells, G., Horwitz, J., & Seetharaman, D. (2021, September 14). Facebook Knows Instagram Is Toxic for Teen Girls, Company Documents Show. WSJ. https://www.wsj.com/articles/facebook- knows-instagram-is-toxic-for-teen-girls-company-documents- show-11631620739

58. Wheeler, T. (2021, April 5). Facebook Says It Supports Internet Regulation. Here's an Ambitious Proposal That Might Actually Make a Difference. Time. https://time.com/5952630/facebook- regulation-agency/

59. Wong, J. C. (2018, March 25). Mark Zuckerberg apologises for Facebook's "mistakes" over Cambridge Analytica. The Guardian. https://www.theguardian.com/technology/2018/ mar/21/mark-zuckerberg-response-facebook-cambridge-analytica

60. Collins, J., & Porras, J., I. (2002, September 1). Built to Last: Successful Habits of Visionary Companies (Harper Business Essentials) (3rd ed.). Collins Business.

61. Dixit, N. (2021, December 10). Fair, But Not So Lovely: India's Obsession With Skin Whitening. Medium. Retrieved September 12, 2022, from https://brightthemag.com/fair-but-not-so-lovely-indias-obsession-with-skin-whitening-beauty-body-image-bleaching-4d6ba9c9743d

62. Lederer, W., Moroz, B., & Warner, C. (2020, August 4). Media Selling: Digital, Television, Audio, Print and Cross-Platform (Fifth). Wiley-Blackwell.

63. Design Matters with Debbie Millman. (n.d.). Spotify. Retrieved September 12, 2022, from https://open.spotify.com/show/4dsmuZLxVGsXpQesSWrebO?si=6c953b3df0984cb2

64. Hidden Brain. (n.d.). Spotify. Retrieved September 12, 2022, from https://open.spotify.com/show/20Gf4IAauFrfj7RBkjcWxh?si=b6ee5df16f654d36

65. HBR IdeaCast. (n.d.). Spotify. Retrieved September 12, 2022, from https://open.spotify.com/show/4gtSBBxIAE142ApX6LqsvN?si=aac34891a27c4e50

66. Your Undivided Attention. (n.d.). Spotify. Retrieved September 12, 2022, from https://open.spotify.com/show/4KI3PtZaWJbAWK89vgttoU?si=6db8602a7cf6401b

67. Making Sense with Sam Harris. (n.d.). Spotify. Retrieved September 12, 2022, from https://open.spotify.com/

show/5rgumWEx4FsqlY8e1wJNAk?si=84ed5a52c2f949ff

68.   Overpriced JPEGs. (n.d.). Spotify. Retrieved September 12, 2022, from https://open.spotify.com/ show/5G2HSDneVg8mZUQ3zUIoLX?si=832c92acdce541a9

69.   Coinbase: Around The Block. (n.d.). Spotify. Retrieved September 12, 2022, from https://open.spotify.com/ show/4QsMNyNEUDu62E3L1PSlWB?si=292b37af6d494f7b

70.   AHAN PENKAR, A. (2022, June 10). *Facebook internal documents reveal Chinese hackers attacking Cambodian opposition party*. The Caravan Magazine. https://caravanmagazine.in/media/ facebook- used-by-chinese-hackers-to-attack-cambodian-government-opposition-hun-sen

We included this piece as it's a deep dive into the meaning of META

(Oglesby, N. D. (n.d.). Facebook and the true meaning of "meta." BBC Future. Retrieved September 12, 2022, from https://www.bbc.com/future/article/20211112-facebook-and-the-true-meaning-of-meta)

Facebook and the true meaning of 'meta'

Prefixes rarely make headlines, but with Facebook's rebrand, "meta" became a word for 2021. Nathan Dufour explores its ancient origins to find out what it says about our present.

In the wake of Facebook's recent rebranding, we've been hearing a lot about the word meta.

Freed from its usual role in English as a prefix in words like "metaphor", "metastasise" and "metamorphosis", it now stands alone as a proper noun, the new name of a social media monolith with the self-declared purpose of ushering its users into the "metaverse".

Meta's metaverse will apparently entail augmented, virtual and mixed reality technologies, to effectuate an immersive online experience – an "embodied internet", where users are not just scrolling, posting and commenting, but interacting in a fully-realised computer-generated world.

Worlds such as this already exist, with games like Minecraft, Roblox and Second Life, which to varying degrees merit the name of "metaverse", depending on whom you ask and how it's being defined. Indeed, much ink (or rather, many a pixel) has recently been spilled over precisely this question – what is a metaverse? And is it a good thing?

But let's explore these questions by asking a more fundamental, and lexical one (a meta-question, if you will): what does the expression meta mean, and what does it symbolise? And what does that have to do with Facebook's new name and vision?

More from the Wise Words series:

- Generational amnesia: The memory loss that harms the planet
- Social cryptomnesia: How societies steal ideas
- The unseen 'slow violence' that affects millions

The term metaverse was coined by Neil Stephenson in his 1992 novel Snow Crash, a speculative epic whose action takes place in two parallel worlds – primary, physical "Reality", and the online, virtual

"Metaverse" existing alongside it. Reality is dominated by malevolent mega-corporations who have privatised every sector of human life, and the Metaverse is fraught with danger, intrigue and corruption.

One may wonder whether this consideration factored into Meta's rebranding process – that the origin of the concept with which they've made themselves synonymous is so distinctly tinged with sci-fi ominousness, and the spectre of worldwide corporatocracy.

But the prefix itself, meta-, was originally an innocent preposition. (Meta is not the first company to appropriate a preposition; I can no longer think of the German über without thinking of taking a ride somewhere.)

It derives from the Greek μετά, which encompasses a wide array of meanings, such as "with", "after", "alongside", "on top of" and "beyond". A metaphor, for instance, is literally an act of carrying (phora) something beyond (meta). In general, meta- can also denote a change of place or state, as in metamorphosis.

One can see how these spatially relational meanings pertain to the recently coined "metaverse" – it refers to a reality existing alongside, upon or beyond the confines of the supposedly primary reality that preexists it, a transcendence of what came before.

But this qualitative aspect of "transcendence" – the connotative aura which makes Meta such a ponderous choice of brand name – did not always attach to the word, and in fact may have glommed onto it only by virtue of an historical accident.

It's from the Greek philosopher Aristotle that we get the term "metaphysics", the branch of philosophy devoted to the most ultimate categories of existence – things like "substance", "being" or "actuality" – which he examines systematically in the work of that name.

Except, that's not what Aristotle himself named the work (which may not have been a finished work at all, so much as a hodgepodge of notes and smaller treatises). Rather, the title seems to have arisen simply because in the traditional ordering of his collected works, it was placed after (meta) another work called the Physics.

Hence, the phrase Meta-physica, meant to merely label "the book after the book about nature (the Physica)", came to refer to the whole philosophical department in which one asks the biggest, broadest questions that can possibly be asked.

It now refers to a conceptual layer of something that is beyond or transcendent of the thing itself

Because of the exalted status of metaphysics (both the book and concept) among the concerns of later Western philosophy, the prefix meta- came to be associated with transcending, comprehending and encompassing. And by extension from that, it now refers to a conceptual layer of something that is beyond or transcendent of the thing itself, and is hence denotes self-awareness or self-reflection.

This shows up in academic discourse, when it gets tacked on to the front of various terms and concepts – metalanguage, metaethics, and so on – when theorists of a given discipline theorise about the parameters of the discipline or concept itself.

Relatedly, in colloquial English, meta has become an adjective, which essentially means extremely self-aware, self-reflective, or self-referential– as in the phrase, "that's so meta". Just as every academic takes a secret delight in the arcane jargon of their discipline's meta-theory, so does each participant in discourse relish the performance of self-awareness that we call meta – everyone wants to be in on the joke.

Memes, for instance, are especially given to meta-reference – their meaning, and their humour, derive from their creators' and viewers' shared awareness of the template's foregoing iterations. It's not a funny picture in and of itself, but because of all the uses of that same picture before it, and the self-aware extra layer that the latest caption lays on top of it. In the age of information, meta-reference is the soul of wit.

It has been the triumph of entertainment franchises to notice that meta-reference and meta-narrative can be commodified. For Meta is not the only company expanding into the metaverse – the same is true for companies like Disney, which owns universes like Star Wars, Marvel and others, into which, as metaverses, they will undoubtedly be inviting their audiences not just as spectators but as participants. (Incidentally, New York Comic Con now offers virtual attendance billed as "Metaverse Membership".)

This very phenomenon was in fact foretold by another metaverse-themed 2011 novel, Ready Player One, made later into a movie – which returns us to the anxieties implicit there and in Snow Crash. For while the user may participate in the metaverse with apparent freedom, they remain subject to those who control the medium itself – the artists and programmers who create that world, and ultimately the powers behind them. Insofar as the simulators control the simulation, they control those who are simulated.

In a sense, this is not far from what companies like Meta have been doing all along. For in giving us spaces in which to create and promulgate our handles, our pages, our brands, they have been luring us into a kind of simulation – one that is characterised not by unity of experience across users, but fragmentation into the pigeon-holes of experience, the selective streams of information, the personalised and curated narratives, that characterise social media.

Our handles, and the whole apparatus by virtue of which we become @ ourselves, rather than being ourselves, represent meta-layers of identity, laid on top of us, and reaching out beyond us. We are beside ourselves.

The opportunity to develop an avatar to represent our (chosen) bodies in virtual space merely makes more literal and vivid a phenomenon that has already been going on – we are already in a metaverse, one in which the storylines run so thick and abundant that unmediated access to the "primary reality" has long since vanished, if indeed it was ever there.

Is the metaverse something that's meant to work beneficially with our world, and our nature? Or are you asking us to pass beyond this world?

The question for Meta then, and for any other company coaxing us into a manifest metaverse, would be, what sense of the word "meta" do you mean?

Is the metaverse something that's meant to work beneficially with our world, and our nature? Or are you asking us to pass beyond this world, as though there's some need to escape what's already here? Do you mean "with, alongside", or do you mean "beyond"?

This connects to a broader technological (and philosophical) question about whether progress consists in "getting beyond" the square one of primary reality – the "beyond" we chase, urged by the illusion of the inadequacy of the here and now. How do our attitudes to that question inform our relationship with the planet, and our use of the internet?

Viewing meta with an even closer etymological lens, we find that it comes from the Proto-Indo-European root element *me-, the same root that goes into the Old English mið, meaning "with" or "among", which is in turn related to the modern English middle.

This may bring the phenomenology of our virtual experience into even sharper relief. For it seems to be the nature of human experience to be in the middle of things, constantly at the fulcrum point between our physical selves and the possibilities of transcendence that are suggested by our consciousness.

We dwell in the middle space between our inherent limitations and the theoretical limitlessness of our technological extensions. And our technologies – like language, writing, telecommunication and virtual reality – have each in turn constituted a metamorphosis in our collective being.

Poised in this middle space, we must consider what kind of -verse we want the metaverse to be. The word "verse" literally implies a turning (from the Latin vertere, to turn) – and so in a cosmological sense, the Universe is a turning-as-one. It remains to be seen whether our metaverses will be a turning-away from that shared movement, and as such a contortion, or a turning-with, and as such a harmony.

An escape, or a genuine connection? Beyond, or alongside? So much hangs upon the use of a preposition.

About The Authors

Amina Qureshi is a global advertising executive, handling marketing for Fortune 500 companies including McDonalds, Rogers and Loblaws. She is currently Head of Financial Services at LinkedIn, helping Canadian big banks to advertise mindfully and responsibly. Her work has appeared in Media in Canada, Digiday and Think with Google. Her recent keynotes include IAB's Report on Data – Digital, Advertising 2.0 and DX3. She is passionate about amplifying female South Asian voices in the advertising industry and has 2,500 followers on LinkedIn. She lives in Toronto, Canada with her husband and young son.

Dona Varghese is Marketing Director and Founder of a full-service marketing agency called DV Media Co. She partners with CEOs, Executives and Solopreneurs to grow their personal and professional brands, human-to-human. Dona Varghese has worked for Media Investment Agencies like MediaCom & Havas Media in the Middle East where she managed tier-one clients like GlaxoSmithKline, LG Electronics and AXA Insurance. Her work has appeared on Think with Google and Facebook Success Stories. She has won numerous industry awards for her work in the Middle East & India. She has also worked in South Africa and New York and currently resides in India.

About The Editor

Ukrainian-born, Canadian-raised **Katrina Petrenko** is a true Citizen of the World, and a Third Culture Kid. The ultimate ingredients for the makings of a word slinger, idea generator and storyteller.

A graduate of OCAD University in Canada with a degree in advertising design, Katrina currently resides in Dubai and specializes in the art of copywriting. A creative director by day, poet by night – author, scriptwriter, adventurer. Katrina's work as a writer and editor is not limited to any medium, format or status quo. From TV commercial scripts to curtain raiser videos, novels, articles and social media content creation, her expertise is valued for its out-of-the-box (sometimes a little big wacky but always on-point) creative perspective.

As a veteran of the advertising industry, the experience of editing Brand New Meta World has inspired Katrina to re-examine her contribution to the marketing machine. "What's next" will be a whole different chapter.

CPSIA information can be obtained
at www.ICGtesting.com
Printed in the USA
BVHW032256061222
653631BV00010B/88